SOCCER SCANDALS

SOCCER SCANDALS

WHEN THE BEAUTIFUL GAME TURNED UGLY

ANTON RIPPON

WHITE OWL
AN IMPRINT OF PEN & SWORD BOOKS LTD.
YORKSHIRE – PHILADELPHIA

First published in Great Britain in 2025 by
PEN AND SWORD WHITE OWL
An imprint of
Pen & Sword Books Ltd
Yorkshire – Philadelphia

ISBN 978 1 39907 910 5

A CIP catalogue record for this book is available from the British Library.

Typeset in Times New Roman 11.5/14 by
SJmagic DESIGN SERVICES, India.
Printed and bound in the UK by CPI Group (UK) Ltd, Croydon, CR0 4YY.

The Publisher's authorised representative in the EU for product safety is
Authorised Rep Compliance Ltd., Ground Floor, 71 Lower Baggot Street,
Dublin D02 P593, Ireland.
www.arccompliance.com

For a complete list of Pen & Sword titles please contact

PEN & SWORD BOOKS LIMITED
George House, Units 12 & 13, Beevor Street, Off Pontefract Road,
Barnsley, South Yorkshire, S71 1HN, England
E-mail: enquiries@pen-and-sword.co.uk
Website: www.pen-and-sword.co.uk

or

PEN AND SWORD BOOKS
1950 Lawrence Rd, Havertown, PA 19083, USA
E-mail: uspen-and-sword@casematepublishers.com
Website: www.penandswordbooks.com

Contents

Contents

Chapter 1

A Disgrace Upon the Country

> A plot to cheat the public, to sell to the faithful followers of football a sham instead of the genuine article, to rob bookmakers by criminal fraud, and to conspire for the suppression of the truth.
>
> *Athletic News*

On Good Friday, 2 April 1915, around 15,000 bedraggled football fans made their way through heavy rain towards Old Trafford for the First Division fixture between Manchester United and Liverpool. Three weeks later the ground, which had opened only five years earlier, would stage an FA Cup Final.

On that occasion almost 50,000 spectators saw Sheffield United beat Chelsea 3-0 in a game which became known as the 'Khaki Cup Final' on account of the number of unformed soldiers in attendance – because Britain was now at war.

That there was an FA Cup competition that season, and a full Football League programme, was surprising. One month before the season began, Germany had declared war on France and entered Belgium, demanding unfettered access to the French border. The Germans refused to remove their troops. Britain, committed to guaranteeing Belgian neutrality and independence, felt it had no option. On 4 August 1914, the First World War was under way. And soon after that so was another football season. Why not? After all, everyone said that this war would be over by Christmas.

Carrying on as usual was not a universally popular decision, however. In November 1914, *The Times* carried a letter from the historian A.H. Pollard: 'Every club that employs a professional football player is bribing a much-needed recruit away from enlistment and every spectator who pays his gate money is contributing so much towards a German victory.'

The FA responded by claiming that 500,000 recruits had already been raised by football organisations, that of 5,000 professionals, some 2,000 were already in the services, and only 600 unmarried professional footballers had failed to heed the call. Some people took exception to claims that football was not supportive of the war effort. Frederick Charrington, heir to an East End brewery fortune who had renounced his inheritance and found his way into the Temperance movement, was given permission by the FA to make a speech on wartime recruitment during the half-time interval of a match at Fulham's Craven Cottage.

For patriots like Charrington – who was regarded by many people as still being one of those grim Victorian philanthropists for whom any entertainment was morally suspect – footballers and their supporters were cowards. No one thought to inform the home club that he had been given permission to air his views. As soon as he began to speak, two Fulham officials set upon him, dragged him down a gangway and threw him out of the ground.

Charrington received a letter from Field Marshall Lord Grenfell who wrote:

> I quite agree with Lord Roberts [a Victorian-era general who was one of the most successful British military commanders of his time] and yourself that professional football, with hostilities going on, and the necessity of every man of suitable age being prepared to go out for the defence of his country, is to be much deprecated … this is not the time for the great football organisations to continue their proceedings.

But continue them they did.

By Easter, however, it was obvious that this would be the players' last as full-time professionals for some time, perhaps for ever. Their livelihoods were about to disappear. Trench warfare on the Western Front had intensified – the Second Battle of Ypres was about to begin – and while some young British men continued to play football, across the Channel many more were dying in the most appalling circumstances.

Nonetheless, the game at Old Trafford on Good Friday was vital to those who still cared. While Liverpool were more or less safe – they would finish midtable, in thirteenth place in the twenty-strong division – Manchester United were still in a desperate fight to avoid dropping into the Second Division.

It was the strangest of games. George Anderson, a Cheetham-born centre-forward who United had bought from Bury for £50 in 1911, opened the scoring after forty minutes. Ten minutes into the second half, United were awarded a penalty but their captain, Irish international Paddy O'Connor, waved Anderson, the usual penalty-taker, away and took the spot-kick himself, hitting it so wide that before play resumed referee John Sharpe of Lichfield and linesman Fred Hargreaves got together to discuss the astonishing miss. Having despatched the ball nearer to the corner-flag than the goal, O'Connor had trotted back with a smile on his face. After sixty-eight minutes, Anderson made it 2-0 before Liverpool's Fred Pagnam appeared to incur the wrath of some of his teammates when he tried a shot which rebounded off the United crossbar.

The sporting press was unimpressed by the afternoon's events, especially by Liverpool's overall feeble attempt at settling their own relegation fears once and for all. The *Sporting Chronicle*'s man at the match thought that if the war itself was not killing football then matches likes this – 'too poor to describe' – would do the job. If a description was needed, however, he said it was 'the most uninteresting game ever seen on the ground which is shortly to see the Final tie'. The *Manchester Courier* reported, 'Play was scrappy, both sides shooting badly … there was not a dangerous forward on the field. Liverpool continued to be overplayed but Manchester could not score again.'

Yet while the game as a poor advertisement for football was commented upon, it would be more than a week before questions were asked publicly about the validity of the result. There had been other surprising results over that Easter weekend, and an absolute sensation on Easter Saturday at Ayresome Park, where table-topping Oldham Athletic lost 4-1 to Middlesbrough. The main talking point of that game, however, was not the result but the astonishing behaviour of Oldham's veteran full-back, the balding, robust Billy Cook. Ten minutes after half-time, Cook – a fine all-round sportsman who had also played first-class cricket for Lancashire – fouled Boro's Jackie Carr. Walter Tinsley scored the resultant penalty to complete the scoring for the afternoon. Ten minutes later Cook clattered Carr again and was sent off. But he refused to leave the field. The referee, Henry Smith of Nottingham, gave the defender a couple of minutes to change his mind but he would not budge. Mr Smith then abandoned the game, Cook was suspended for twelve months, the game was not replayed, the result stood and Oldham finished runners-up, one point behind champions Everton.

Manchester United, meanwhile, embarked on a dreadful run, losing at Newcastle, Bradford Park Avenue, Oldham and Sheffield United, and drawing at home to Middlesbrough before winning their last two games, at Chelsea and home to Aston Villa. Those final four points were enough to see them finish in eighteenth place, one point ahead of Chelsea and two in front of bottom club Tottenham Hotspur. Chelsea would have particular reason to feel aggrieved. The Old Trafford match that had gifted Manchester United two points was about betting, not United's survival in the First Division. When all the investigations into it were concluded, the result itself would be allowed to stand.

Eight days after Liverpool's Good Friday visit to Old Trafford, the *Sporting Chronicle* ventured to suggest that the result had left football followers 'cold with stupefaction'. Fans did not know what to think. It was now only a matter of time, and it did not take long. The *Sporting Chronicle* published a notice from a firm of bookmakers who signed themselves 'The Football Kings'.

It read:

> We have solid grounds for believing that a certain First League match played in Manchester during Easter weekend was 'squared', the home club being permitted to win by a certain score. Further, we have information that several of the players of both teams invested substantial sums on naming the correct score of this match with our firm and others. Such being the case, we wish to inform all our clients and the football public generally that we are withholding payment on these correct score transactions, also that we are causing searching investigations to made with the object of punishing the instigators of this reprehensible conspiracy. With this object in view, we are anxious to receive reliable information bearing on the subject, and we will willingly pay the substantial reward named above to anyone giving information which will lead to the punishment of the offenders.

The reward offered was £50. The odds on a score of 2-0 had been 7/1.

On 24 April, the day of the FA Cup Final, it appeared that the football authorities had reacted immediately. A statement said that a Football League commission had already been appointed but it was withholding 'any report at present', pointing out that 'the allegations referred to are not made in connection with any particular match, and may refer to either of two'.

Whoever was involved, the statement warned:

> If, as stated therein, direct bets have been made by players, such conduct is contrary rules of the FA and, in accordance with declarations the FA and the Football League, any such player found guilty would be put out football for ever. The conspiracy alleged is a criminal offence, upon which the aggrieved parties can take action.

The statement went on:

> If the injured parties are not prepared so to act and will furnish us with any information justifying such allegations, or either of them, we are prepared to pursue our inquiries to the utmost, and fearlessly impose adequate punishment … There is one further alternative. If the party responsible for the issue of the coupon referred to will publicly state the match referred to and furnish us with his name and address, thus accepting responsibility for the publication of such coupon, the twenty-two players concerned will immediately take action for libel and test the whole question in the courts before a judge and jury. If this challenge is not accepted within fourteen days we shall know what construction to place on the anonymous allegations, and shall issue a further report based upon our investigations. (Signed) J. Lewis, H. Keys, C.E. Sutcliffe.

Charles Sutcliffe, a lawyer, had played for Burnley before taking up refereeing and was the founder and first president of the Referees' Association. John Lewis had been involved in the formation of Blackburn Rovers and was an international referee who would take charge of the 1920 Olympic Final. All three men were members of the Football League management committee.

The enquiry into the Good Friday match was already well under way. Despite the League's demand that Football Kings should identify the match in question, it was already obvious. Several players had already been interviewed. They included two United players, goalkeeper Bobby Beal and half-back Arthur Whalley (who had not played in the game) and Liverpool forward Jackie Sheldon, a former United player.

The three-man enquiry held its first official meeting at the Grand Hotel in Manchester on 10 May. There was no immediate news. Reports said that the panel had travelled around, collecting evidence. They would not be rushed into publishing their findings.

During the summer months, more players were interviewed. They included Manchester United's 'Welsh wizard' of a winger Billy Meredith, who in 1905, when he was with title-chasing Manchester City, had been one of seventeen players banned from playing for City ever again – several directors were also suspended and City's manager, Tom Maley, banned sine die – after a match against Aston Villa in which Meredith was alleged to have offered Villa's Alex Leake £10 to throw the final game of the season. Leake refused the offer, Villa won 3-2, and City finished third in the First Division (Newcastle United won 3-0 at Middlesbrough that day and would have taken the title even if City had won at Villa Park). Before the end of his eighteen-month suspension Meredith had joined rivals Manchester United. Three other suspended City players – Sandy Turnbull, Herbert Burgess and Jimmy Bannister – joined him at United's Bank Street ground.

In October 1904, City had been fined £250, its Hyde Road ground closed for a month, one player suspended, three directors banned from football for three years, and the financial director suspended for life, after being found guilty of paying illegal inducements to players, far in excess of the £10 permitted. The 1905 bribery attempt had again brought in the FA who uncovered evidence of yet more illegal payments of wages and bonuses. This time City's entire first-team squad was banned.

Ten years later, however, Meredith would not be implicated in the Manchester United-Liverpool match-fixing accusation. As the 1915–16 season dawned, football was now on a wartime regional footing, the Football League proper and the FA Cup suspended for the duration.

And still there was no news of the commission's findings into the events of 2 April that year. The FA was also now involved and the enquiry met again in October, and again in November. A verdict was promised for Friday, 17 December 1915 but the assembled journalists were disappointed: there had been a disagreement among the panel's members and its report would have to be delayed.

Finally, on 23 December, it was made public. It read:

> Manchester United v Liverpool, 2 April 1915
>
> The commission appointed first by the Football League, and afterwards the Football Association, have fully investigated rumours and allegations largely circulated in several districts during and immediately after the above match, to the effect that the result was pre-arranged for the purpose of betting and winning money thereby.
>
> A mass of information was received. The allegation of squaring the match carried with it a charge of conspiracy by some of the players, and as a result of long and searching investigations we are satisfied that a number of them were party to arrangements to do so, and joined together to obtain money by betting on the actual result of match.
>
> It is proved that a considerable sum of money changed hands by betting on the match, and that some of the players profited thereby. Every opportunity has been given to the players to tell the truth, but although they were warned that the commissioners were in possession of those facts, some have persistently refused to do so, thus revealing a conspiracy to keep back the truth.
>
> It is almost incredible that players dependent on the game for their livelihood have resorted to such base tactics. By their action they have sought to undermine the whole fabric of the game and discredit its honesty and fairness. We are bound to view such offences in a serious light. The honesty and uprightness of the game must be preserved at all costs, and although we sympathise greatly with the clubs, who are bound to suffer seriously, we feel we have no alternative but to impose the punishments of which the players have been warned over and over again would be imposed.

> We are satisfied that the allegations have been proved against the players J. Sheldon, R.R. Pursell, T. Miller and T. Fairfoul (Liverpool), A. Turnbull. A. Whalley and E.A. West (Manchester United), L. Cook (Chester).
>
> And they are, therefore, permanently suspended from taking part in football or football management and shall not be allowed to enter any football ground in the future.
>
> There are grave suspicions that others are also involved, but as the penalty is severe we have restricted our findings to those as to whose offence there is no reasonable doubt.
>
> F. Howard (Manchester City) is suspended until the expiration of twelve months after the registration of professional players has been resumed by the Football Association for the unsatisfactory and contradictory manner in which he gave evidence before the commission.
>
> There has never been the slightest allegation against the clubs or their officials. It is, therefore, unnecessary to exonerate them from blame or conspiracy and we are indebted to them for much assistance in our investigations.

And there it was. But there were unanswered questions. Why was only one Manchester United player actually in that team – Enoch 'Knocker' West – suspended? Surely he could not have helped to contrive the result without the aid of at least some of his teammates? Was Manchester City centre-forward Fred Howard – who, along with Chester centre-forward and Lancashire cricketer Lol Cook, was one of the players from other clubs involved who apparently benefited from the betting fraud – really the only one who gave unsatisfactory and contradictory answers to the commission? And why did Paddy O'Connell hit that penalty-kick so wide that it ended up by the corner-flag? Was he in on the plan and thought it too early to score the second goal? Or was he trying to thwart the plotters?

By now Jackie Sheldon was serving on the Western Front with the 17th (Service) Battalion, Middlesex Regiment, the famous 'Football Battalion'. When the suspension were lifted after the war, Sheldon, a goal-scoring outside-right, would play for Liverpool for a further two seasons. He would also play a major part in the aftermath of the Good Friday scandal. Full-back Bob Pursell had already been involved in footballing irregularities; when they signed him from Scottish club Queen's Park in 1911, Liverpool had overlooked the legal niceties. He, too, was allowed to play again after the war, although he managed only two more appearances for Liverpool. Scotsmen Tom Fairfoul, a half-back, and centre-forward Tom Miller had both played for Liverpool in the 1914 FA Cup Final defeat by Burnley. After 1915, Fairfoul's career with the Anfield club was over but Miller returned to make a further twenty-nine League and FA Cup appearances before moving, ironically perhaps, to Manchester United in 1921. By the time the commission report was published Miller, like Sheldon, was also serving in the army.

Of the Manchester United men suspended, Alex 'Sandy' Turnbull, yet another Scot, was one of the Manchester City players banned by the FA in 1905 over an illegal payments scandal, and who played for United once their suspensions were lifted. His goals had helped United to two League titles. Sandy Turnbull was serving with the East Surrey Regiment when he was killed during the Battle of Arras in May 1917. His body was never formally identified and he is commemorated on the Arras memorial. Half-back Arthur Whalley, who, like Turnbull, did not play in the Good Friday match, would survive being seriously wounded at Passchendaele and play Third Division football until the 1926–27 season, after which he worked, again perhaps ironically, as a bookmaker.

Which left Enoch 'Knocker' West, who had scored almost 100 goals for Nottingham Forest before United signed him for the start of the 1910–11 season. He scored eighty goals in 181 League and FA Cup appearances for United before he began what turned out to be a suspension that would not be lifted for thirty years.

With a war raging, it was not surprising that the sensational events at Old Trafford on Good Friday 1915 were now no longer making news. The guilty players, or at least some of them, had been publicly named and punished. There were much bigger battles to fight, not least the one that began on 1 July 1916 on the Somme. In April, however, the *Liverpool Echo* reported that a letter had been received from Private J. Sheldon of the 'Football Battalion'. Sheldon was serving in France but found time to write the following:

> Would you kindly grant me space in your valuable paper to explain my position re suspension? Perhaps it is unfair for me to ask this favour after my case has been dealt with so

> long ago by the FA. But you will understand how difficult it is for me to explain while doing my bit 'Somewhere in France'. I am now taking the first opportunity I have had, and wish to let the numerous followers of football know how I stand. I emphatically state to you as our best and fairest critic, that I am absolutely blameless in this scandal, and am still open, as I have always been, to give any Red Cross Fund or any other charitable institution the sum of £20 if the FA, or anyone else, can bring forward any bookmaker or any other person with whom I have had a bet. Assuming I return safely from this country, I intend to take action against my suspension, and in the meantime you would do me a great favour if you would kindly insert this letter in your issue. Begging to remain, yours faithfully, Private J Sheldon 17th Middlesex.

The *Liverpool Echo* commented: 'E.J. West, it is common knowledge, has taken up a similar attitude, and he has been in communication with the Football Association.'

Enoch West, who was now working at the Ford works on the Trafford Park industrial estate, was going to do much more than simply appeal to the FA. And Jackie Sheldon was going to bring about his ultimate downfall.

After appearing outside Old Trafford – he was of course, banned from entering the ground – before a Lancashire Section game between Manchester United and Liverpool, and handing out leaflets printed in the same style as the 'Football Kings' notices of 1915 and offering £50 to anyone could prove he had made money from the Good Friday game, in July 1917 Enoch West went to court, claiming damages for libel from the FA and from newspaper publishers E. Hulton and Co. Up to a point the evidence seemed to give West the benefit of the doubt. Then entered Jackie Sheldon.

The author of the letter protesting his innocence now confessed. He was the ringleader of the plot to swindle the bookies. And on the Monday before that game he had met his former Manchester United teammate, Sandy Turnbull, Arthur Whalley and, yes, Enoch West, in the Dog and Partridge pub. There the four of them agreed to fix the result of the Good Friday match at 2-0 in United's favour. Sheldon would sort out his Liverpool teammates. On the eve of the game, it was agreed that there would be one goal scored in each half. Once the score was 2-0, Sheldon told the court, United players then ignored Billy Meredith (who later said that he wondered why no one would pass the ball to him) and fed West, who promptly kicked the ball into touch.

Then George Anderson, scorer of United's two goals in the match, gave evidence. On the Thursday before the game, he had met West and two others at the Great Central Station in Manchester. Sheldon joined them in a nearby pub. One of the men asked: 'Is it still two-nil?' Anderson said that West replied: 'Oh yes. I've just written to Nottingham for £70 to £10.' Anderson said that he was offered £3 to join in the arrangement but had refused. Sheldon told him to remain silent. After the game, said Anderson, West told him: 'I'm not afraid. They can't get any evidence against me.' Anderson admitted that he had denied any knowledge of the arrangement to fix the result but, eventually: 'I was tired of telling so many lies.'

More witnesses piled in, and it was no surprise when the judge summed up. He said that he considered the reports to be 'fair comment' and merely reflected the facts stated in the FA's final judgement.

Mr Justice Ridley, who tried the case, said:

> This is a case in which a football match which has drawn great attention from the public in Lancashire has been squared in the most fraudulent manner, which is a shame and a disgrace upon this country, and particularly upon the place where it occurred. I think the language used is not too strong.

West, though, would not let the matter go. In February 1918, the Court of Appeal agreed to a new trial on the question of whether the newspaper reports had libelled him. His right to appeal against the FA ban was refused.

In January 1919, West again lost his case against the newspapers. Quite how he had found the money to finance both trials was one question that puzzled many. His persistence cost him too. Unlike the others who had taken their punishment, West remained suspended from all football until the FA's general amnesty in October 1945.

In April 1918, George Anderson, the man tired of telling lies about the Good Friday 1915 plot, was found guilty of conspiring with persons unknown to defraud people of money wagered upon football matches. These involved games between Everton and Blackpool, and Oldham Athletic and Blackburn Rovers. His trial at Liverpool Assizes lasted three days; the jury took only one hour to reach their verdict. Anderson was sentenced to eight months' imprisonment with hard labour. He seemed 'very much distressed when the jury found him guilty'.

In passing sentence, Mr Justice Salter, who also happened to be the Conservative MP for Basingstoke, said that Anderson's conduct was disgraceful: 'It is very bad at this time, when the very existence of the country is at stake, that any man should be playing football at all, and it is worse that people should be betting on it.'

Many people were disappointed for all sorts of reasons. After the suspensions were announced, the *Oxford Chronicle and Reading Gazette* commented:

> Amongst Oxford city and county footballers there will be no sympathy for the eight one-time professionals who have been suspended by a Commission of the Football Association and the League from all further participation in football or football management. Their offence was that, for purpose of betting, they 'faked' the League match Manchester United v Liverpool, played on 2 April of last season. After a thorough investigation of the case the Commission had no doubt as to the guilt – complicity is too mild a word to use – of eight of the players, and their definite exclusion from football in the future is the result. They have got off lightly, too. What can one think of professional football when such a thing is not only possible but is actually carried out? There have been longings in the past for a 'pro team' for Oxford, but even had it been possible to run one here, people were agreed that it would have been undesirable, and those happenings at Manchester last spring will strengthen that opinion. Football as a sport is the finest game ever invented; but football as a business – well, evidently it isn't football at all …
>
> In Monday's *Athletic News*, in a long discussion of the case, one finds the following: 'Does not this exposure

> indirectly suggest the wisdom of insisting upon a law that the man who plays football for money must at the same time work for his livelihood? Wages from football should be supplementary and not the support of any man.'
>
> That would be a step in the right direction. But would it not be still better, when peace comes round again, that the rules that have been in force this winter shall continue to prevail – that no man shall, under any circumstances, receive money for playing football? If he is at work throughout the week, his Saturday afternoon football is a sport and recreation, and temptations such as assailed the players in the match in question could hardly arise. The most satisfactory point of the whole affair, however, is the knowledge that the English Football Association and League are determined to do their utmost to ensure that football as presented by professionals shall be honest and pure.

There was a suggestion in some quarters that it would be a good idea to scrap the maximum wage rule and legitimately pay footballers more money, and then they would not be tempted to manipulate results for their own gain. It would be more than forty years before that happened. And even then …

Chapter 2

A Dishonest Charade

> Pay the man a handsome rate for the job while he is doing it and let him take care of his own future when his career is over. Then you will not have these miserable stories about bribes.
>
> Ferenc Puskas, Real Madrid and Spain

On 7 April 1963, *The People* newspaper carried a story headlined '£100,000 Soccer Bribes Coup'. One might have expected such a piece to have made the front page, especially when one considers that this equates to more than £2.6 million today. But the article was tucked away on the bottom of page eleven, alongside a report that striptease girl Rusty Gaynor was taking out a writ for libel against David Frost, compere of BBC's Saturday night satire show *That Was The Week That Was*, and a story concerning Mrs Dorothy Hubbard of Swaything, near Southampton, who complained that twenty 'beatniks' were holding 'wild drinking parties' in a farmyard at the bottom of her garden.

In truth, the soccer betting coup story was less hard fact and more conjecture by unhappy bookmakers who had lost heavily after accepting double bets on the results of two Football League matches the previous day, where Stockport County and Derby County had both been heavily backed to win at home. Both clubs did just that. Stockport beat Hartlepool United 4-1 in a Fourth Division match at Edgeley Park, and Derby hammered Scunthorpe United in a Second Division fixture at the Baseball Ground. Neither result was particularly unusual. Hartlepool were rock bottom of the table, while Scunthorpe were only just above Derby. Indeed, Derby had been involved in far more remarkable results; on Easter Monday 1958, for instance, the Rams beat Swansea Town 1-0 at home, and then, twenty-fours later, managed to lose 7-0 to the Swans at Vetch Field. There was no suggestion of murky goings on then. It was simply one of those wonderful, inexplicable idiosyncrasies of football which is why we love the game. More importantly, there was no betting on such a freak result.

Five years later, it was a different matter. At odds of 6/4 on both clubs winning at home, bets of between £50 and £1,000 a time had placed at the same time all over Britain. Anxious bookies had tried to lay-off the wagers, and by the Friday afternoon it was impossible to bet on the two games. Norwich-based turf accountant Jack Pointer, who had refused to take big bets because, he claimed, he had been hit by similar coups in the past, summed up the feelings of many in his profession: 'There is likely to be such a stink that this time the Football League will have to investigate.'

The League's initial reaction, however, was that there was 'nothing to see here'. Its secretary, Alan Hardaker, said: 'The truth of the matter is that bookies are nowhere near as smart as they like to think. If they choose to include matches that even a four-year-old can pick the winner of their fixed-odds coupons, that is their look-out.'

Fixed odds betting on the results of football matches had been around for forty years or more, but it was in the immediate post-war years – the game's so-called 'golden age' – when an average of 39 million fans passed through the turnstiles each season that it began to generate serious income for national bookmakers and pools companies. When on-street betting was legalised in 1961 smaller bookies 'borrowed' the odds and joined in the boom. The odds for selecting the correct result for two games are obviously greater than those for a single match.

Between the wars there had been disciplinary punishments for fixing the results of matches but these had been mostly concerned with players bribing opponents to let their team win in a bid to gain promotion or avoid relegation. In the fifteen years after the war, there had been only rumours of match-fixing, although in his 1957 autobiography *I Lead the Attack*, the fiery Wales international centre-forward Trevor Ford was not shy in talking about it publicly.

Ford cited the case of a game where it was decided that the captain of one team would approach his opposite number, offering £5 to every member of the visiting side if they would 'sell' the game. The opposing skipper was only too ready to cooperate but when the home team manager was asked if he could arrange for £55 to be made available, he turned the request down flat.

It was not the only case, said Ford:

> There are many more and most of them centre on relegation. How often have you seen a club requiring a couple of points from the last match of the season win by umpteen goals to one? … It happens time and again, and you won't be far wrong if you reason that the viper of bribery had reared its ugly head again.
>
> The cankers to our game come and go. They're to be found at all levels, as much at the top as anywhere … the grand inquisitor will not find all the guilty in the dressing-rooms. He'll have to haul his dragnet through the offices and boardrooms.

Ford had also confessed to receiving 'under-the-counter' payments from Sunderland's directors to overcome the maximum wage legislation still in force in football. In April 1957, the Wearsiders, not for nothing known as 'the Bank of England club', were fined a record £5,000. Three directors faced sine die bans after wholesale illegalities were uncovered.

Manager Bill Murray was also fined and he resigned, ending a twenty-eight-year association with Sunderland as a player and coach. When, on the advice of their union's lawyers, five players – Ray Daniel, Ken Chisholm, Billy Elliott, Willie Fraser and Johnny Hannigan – remained silent in front of a joint FA and Football League Commission, they condemned themselves to also receiving bans. In April 1962, in the High Court, the five players each received an undisclosed sum of damages, in return withdrawing charges of conspiracy against members of the Commission. Daniel said: 'Now we are at last cleared of the allegations and suspicions that we were tainted characters. We are to get back all the money we lost.'

Three years after Ford's book was published the public were given a glimpse of how the 'viper' had poisoned the national game. In September 1960, the Football League announced that it was investigating a report from Stoke City that their goalkeeper, Jimmy O'Neill, a Republic of Ireland international, had received an offer of money to facilitate Stoke losing their home game against Norwich City on 27 August that year.

A spokesman for the Stoke club said:

> On the evening before the Stoke and Norwich game, O'Neill, a player of the highest character, who joined our club this season [from Everton for a £5,000 transfer fee] had a telegram asking him to ring a phone in a town in the West Country. The telegram purported to be sent by a footballer who is known to O'Neill.
>
> O'Neill phoned the number given in the telegram which was a call box. A man answered and asked O'Neill if he was interested in making some money by ensuring that Stoke lost to Norwich.
>
> O'Neill said the match was only the next day and the man then suggested he might consider a similar proposition for a future Stoke match.

Ten minutes after that telephone call O'Neill reported the circumstances to Stoke's manager, Tony Waddington.

The Potters issued a statement: 'The Stoke directors considered the matter and sent detailed reports to the Football League and to the Stoke-on-Trent CID. On their joint advice the bribe incident was treated by the club in strict confidence while investigations were made.'

Stoke-on-Trent CID issued its own short statement: 'The facts given by the Stoke City club are substantially correct. Police inquiries are continuing but no person has been charged.'

The Stoke-Norwich game ended in a 1-1 draw, and a month later both the football authorities and the newspapers were looking for the fixers. It was the newspapers who would lead the way.

On Friday 14 October 1960, the *Daily Mail* carried a story that had nothing to do with betting but everything to do with match-fixing. Exeter City's player-manager Glen Wilson claimed that, in April 1958, when he was with Brighton, he played in two Third Division South games against Watford where there was an arrangement between players from both clubs to let Brighton – who were in contention for promotion – win. Watford, meanwhile, were almost certain to drop into the newly created Fourth Division for 1958–59.

His account was backed up by Watford's former captain, Johnny Meadows, who told the newspaper: 'Some other Watford players and myself shared £100 between us from the Brighton players at the end of the season to "bend"' a home and away match with them.' Meadows seemed unconcerned with the morals of the arrangement: 'We wouldn't have beaten them anyway.'

Although Watford's fate was all but sealed – they needed to win their two remaining games and even then hope that Colchester United lost their last game – Brighton were desperate for the points. Along with Swindon Town, Plymouth Argyle and Brentford they were fighting for the single promotion place to the Second Division. Swindon and Plymouth each had one game left, Brentford two, Brighton three.

It was an unusual season anyway. The Football League was restructuring. Clubs that finished in the bottom half of the Third Division South would be relegated into a new Fourth Division along with clubs in the lower half of the Third Division North.

On the last Saturday, Brighton won at Watford 1-0, the goal coming in the final minute of the game. Watford's manager, Neil McBain, felt there was something odd about the game. He suspected that someone had been 'got at'.

Brighton were now joint top of the table with two games in hand on Plymouth, who had completed their fixtures. On the Monday, Brighton lost at Brentford, which saw Brentford go top. It came down to Brighton's final game two days later – at home to Watford.

Now there was another interested party. There were claims that Jimmy Bowie, a former Watford and Brentford player, had offered money to Johnny Meadows to incentivise a Watford win. And that Meadows had rejected the offer because Brighton had offered more to Watford to lose the match.

At the Goldstone Ground on 30 April 1958, Brighton were 3-0 ahead after only eleven minutes, thanks to a hat-trick from a 20-year-old reserve-team striker, former Brighton Grammar School boy Adrian Thorne, who was making only his seventh first-team appearance. Thorne went on to score five that evening and Brighton won promotion to the Second Division with a 6-0 victory. Glen Wilson scored the other goal from the penalty spot before 29,454 mostly happy spectators.

Wilson assured the *Daily Mail*: 'It was between some of the players alone. The club managements knew nothing about it but I don't want to say any more about it. This sort of thing happens all the time.'

On the day that *Daily Mail* article appeared, Wilson arrived at an Oldham hotel along with the rest of his Exeter team for a match at Boundary Park the following day. He went straight to his room, refusing to discuss the bribery allegations with waiting journalists. Only after telephoning the Exeter City chairman, George Gillin, did he came down to face the reporters.

He told them:

> I've nothing to say now about the reports that have appeared. All I need is three or four days and I'll get the whole thing straightened out. The whole business has made my wife ill and I want to get it sorted out as soon as possible. But I will say that I am clean.

George Gillin, who had remained in Exeter, described the story as 'distressing', and Wilson's brother, Joe, who was Brighton's trainer, said: 'I just can't believe that this can be true'.

Brighton's manager, Billy Lane, said that when he first heard of the *Daily Mail*'s story he thought that 'someone must be playing a joke'. He said that five players who appeared in the matches against Watford and who were still with Brighton 'wish it to be known that they are no way implicated and protest about it'.

Johnny Meadows said: 'I'm in enough trouble at the moment, so don't ask me anything more.' He need not have worried. Although the Football Association and the Football League announced that they would meet at the FA offices in London in two days' time, no action was ever taken against anyone allegedly involved in the fixing of the matches between Brighton and Watford.

The *Daily Mail*'s investigations, however, continued. The newspaper had four reporters – Michael Borissow, Bernard Jordan, Robert Greaves and Harold Pendlebury – digging deeper into reports of bribery and corruption on and off the football pitch. *The People*, too, was doing more than football's ruling bodies to uncover corruption in the game. On 9 October 1960, the former Swansea Town, Manchester City and Wales international wing-half, Roy Paul, revealed in the newspaper that he had been paid to lose matches.

Paul, now 37 years old and player–coach of Welsh League Third Division club Garw Athletic in Glamorgan, claimed that he had pocketed £500 to throw matches. In typical Sunday tabloid revelation fashion, no doubt aided by a ghost writer, he told readers: 'I've been a soccer wide boy. And, like most soccer wide boys, I believed there was one set of rules for the next man – and one for me.'

He said that the reason he accepted bribes was simple: where many other clubs were happy to pay under-the-counter payments to players transferred, augment bonuses well above what was allowed, and pay 'nicely timed drops' to players who were hesitating to re-sign their contracts, Manchester City (unlike in Edwardian days) were cleaner than a referee's whistle: 'But I wanted cash – more cash than I was paid. So if Manchester City weren't going to pay it to me, I argued with a sort of Robin Hood reasoning, I had to find it elsewhere.'

Paul said that when he was desperate for money, he twice sold matches. 'Not packets in the street but matches in which Manchester City played. I took dough to see we lost.'

On the first occasion, he said, he collected £500 from the manager's office of a club desperate for points to avoid relegation. The money was on a desk – '£500 in single notes … in a neat brown paper parcel done up with string.' He shared the ill-gotten gains with a teammate who was also in on the secret 'not to try too hard'. On the second occasion the player that had shared the money with Paul took it upon himself to fix another match. Most of the players in on the arrangement received £5, but after Paul threatened to tell the Manchester City manager, Les McDowell, his share of the bribe money was increased to £25. He refused to name any of the other players involved: 'They are still earning their living from the game.'

Eric Westwood, a former Manchester City full-back who had been mentioned in dispatches while serving in the Manchester Regiment during the Second World War, was incensed at Paul's claims. Now a publican in Manchester, Westwood told a *Manchester Evening News* reporter that he wanted to get all the players together and confront Paul:

> I'll pay his expenses if he can't afford the fare. Each player could get up and ask him, 'Did I ever receive any money?' He would have to answer 'Yes' or 'No.' … Some players say that they do not believe what Paul said about accepting bribes. Knowing Paul as I do, I am willing to believe every word – except his allegations about the £5 share-out.

The floodgates might not have opened yet, but there was still a steady drip of 'confessions'. One, only two days after the Roy Paul story broke, came as quite a shock when the former Scotland and Celtic centre-half

Bobby Evans, who was winding down his career with Chelsea, told to the *Daily Mail* that he had once offered Everton's Alex Parker, a fellow Scot, £500 to lose an Everton v Chelsea match. Parker was not interested: Everton won the match 6-1. However, the 32-year-old Evans, who won forty-eight international caps and made more than 500 appearances for Celtic, said that it was nothing more than a foolish practical joke. He had never made any bets himself and had never been involved in match-fixing. A former Celtic teammate, Charlie Tully, said:

> I know that Bobby wrote a lot of silly articles when he left Celtic. But when I played with him he was one of the nicest boys you could meet, a really good boy who never put a penny on the dogs or horses. If the bribery story is true, it must have happened after he moved south. In all my career I have never come into any bribery myself.

Hard on the heels of the Evans claim, the *News Chronicle* revealed 'the biggest bribe in the football fixing scandal' when Bury's South African-born outside-left Johnny Hubbard said that he had been offered £6,000 to fix the Barnsley v Bury match the previous February. Hubbard said that he was offered £3,000 for himself and £3,000 to share among his teammates. The offer allegedly came from 'a big betting syndicate' through an unnamed Scottish First Division player. Hubbard immediately informed the Bury management. The Shakers' manager, Dave Russell, told the newspaper: 'A fellow from Glasgow had an interview with Hubbard. Johnny came to see me and said he had been offered this money. We told him to let the matter drop.'

John Higgins, a centre-half who had played for Bolton Wanderers against Manchester United in the 1958 FA Cup Final and whose career was coming to a premature end at the age of 27, claimed that he had been offered £200 to lose a home game against Manchester City. Higgins refused and at half-time, when the score was 1-1, the offer was doubled. Higgins still was not interested and Bolton won the game 3-1. Higgins said that the initial approach had been made at Manchester's Continental Club. He had treated the offer of a bribe as a joke but then the same player approached him at the ground.

Then came a report that the approaches to Higgins and to Jimmy O'Neill had been made separately by men who had played with the Liverpool clubs in the 1950s, who were now with the same club, and who lived in the same lodgings. On 10 October, newspapers reported that Higgins had denied an alleged statement that Roy Saunders, the Swansea Town and former Liverpool midfielder, had been the man who had offered him £200 to see that Bolton lost at Burnden Park on 18 April 1960. The player who had spoken to O'Neill told the *Daily Mail* that the Stoke goalkeeper had misunderstood their conversation: 'I have never bet on a football match in my life. I don't even understand fixed odds betting.'

Throughout the 1960–61 season, reports of matching-fixing over the previous season and into the current one built up into a worrying picture about the state of the national game. One letter alleged that a West Ham United player had three times received £1,000 to facilitate defeats for the Hammers. On 20 February 1960, Newcastle United's surprise 5-3 win at Upton Park had been under suspicion as it was coupled in a fixed odds bet with Grimsby Town's surprise win at Brentford the same day.

On 23 April 1960, there were more suspect games, notably when Manchester United, unbeaten in their previous five games, lost 5-2 to Arsenal who were enduring a poor run of form. Other games that raised concerns that day were: Swansea Town 1, Derby County 2; Bolton Wanderers 2, Chelsea 0; Nottingham Forest 3, Newcastle United 0.

The Football League's public face on the matter was that most of the allegations received by them were untrue.

On 12 October, the *Manchester Evening News* reporter Eric Thornton said that Alan Hardaker, the Football League secretary, seemed 'more shy and evasive than ever and provided little satisfaction' when he was questioned. In his later autobiography, Hardaker, said that 'the Law and the League could not get the evidence to nail' the guilty men. It was true. After sending their findings to the Director of Public Prosecutions, the FA and the Football League were advised that there was insufficient evidence to mount prosecutions. Anonymous letters were not enough.

Yet still the rumours persisted. On 21 October 1961, away wins for Tranmere Rovers at York, and for Bradford City at Mansfield commanded fixed odds of 10/1 as a double bet. Tranmere and Bradford had each previously won only one away game that season, and York and Mansfield both boasted good home records. One Mansfield supporter wrote to say that the game at Field Mill was 'full of strange incidents'.

Furthermore, many bets, including several placed in Yorkshire, had been made by someone with the same surname, as well as by several clients new to the bookmakers concerned. Twelve individuals had placed bets on these matches with twenty different gambling organisations. Winnings were withheld.

The *Daily Mail* investigations not only continued to turn up alleged instances of bribes being offered to players to fix the results of matches, they also found that a world-famous referee had been approached. Arthur Ellis, from Halifax, whose fame later extended to the BBC television game show *It's A Knockout*, said that he had once turned down £35 to help bring about a particular result.

The Professional Footballers' Association (PFA) was becoming increasingly concerned about the allegations. Under the chairmanship of Fulham's Jimmy Hill, the PFA was on the brink of forcing the Football League to end its controversial maximum wage rule. If the main reason for footballers accepting bribes was that they could not earn more money from the game by legitimate means, then that could surely be no bad thing. The rule was abolished in January 1961 and Hill's Fulham teammate Johnny Haynes, the England captain, became the British game's first £100-a-week player. Quite a decent rise from the £20 maximum that had been in operation since 1958.

Meanwhile, Littlewoods lent the Football League the services of two former police officers to interview twelve punters in particular. Most were considered innocent and after their cheques were stopped, eleven of them did not claim their winnings. The odd man out was Jimmy Gauld, a 32-year-old Scot whose football career with Mansfield Town was in doubt after he suffered a broken leg. The investigators' conclusion was that although Gauld presented as a shrewd and sharp-witted individual, there was no evidence linking him to match-fixing. In February 1965, Alan Hardaker said that when he interviewed Gauld, in the presence of the Mansfield Town chairman and manager at the Football League headquarters at Lytham St Annes on 29 November 1961, after the Littlewoods-backed investigation had ended, 'despite the fact that he denied any wrongdoing … the final impression was that he was not telling the truth'. The League's findings were handed to Lancashire County Police but Hardaker said that 'it was not possible to make much progress in the investigations until the first confession was made through Bristol Rovers to the Football Association and to the League'.

That confession had come in 1963, the year that the Beatles exploded on Britain, Martin Luther King Junior told the world, 'I have a dream',

President John Kennedy was assassinated, and Britain's secretary of state for war became embroiled with a model and a Soviet military attaché, and thus the Profumo Scandal held the nation's attention.

There was another scandal, of particular interest to football fans. On 28 April 1963, three weeks after *The People* had hidden its '£100,000 Soccer Bribes Coup' story on page eleven, the front-page lead of 'The Paper That Looks Ahead' was headlined: 'SOCCER BRIBE SENSATION'.

Bristol Rovers' goalkeeper Esmond Million confessed that he had accepted a £300 bribe to lose a Third Division match against Bradford at Park Avenue eight days earlier.

Journalist Mike Kiddey reported that while 'the goalkeeper's attractive wife, Margaret', played with the couple's 2-year-old son, Mark, in their club house in Reynolds Drive, Horfield, Bristol, 25-year-old Million stretched out on a settee and told the reporter 'the story that will rock the football world'.

'It all started with a phone call from a friend on the Tuesday before the Bradford match,' he said. The friend was acting as a go-between on behalf of someone who wanted Bradford to win. Million said that it 'took a lot of heart-searching' because he loved football. But he also had money troubles. The couple's previous home, a bungalow in Middlesbrough, was proving difficult to sell. On the eve of the game, the Bristol Rovers players – who had won only three of their last nineteen away games – travelled up to Doncaster where they spent the night in a hotel and where Million had arranged to meet his friend at the Yorkshire town's main railway station.

'He handed me a first instalment of £50 in fivers. He told me, "We want Bradford to win. If they lose we want our money back."'

Million said he had the impression that he was dealing with a tough crowd. But it was too late to back down. And things did not go to plan. In the first half at Park Avenue, Bristol twice went ahead, forcing him into two blatant errors to drew the home side level again. First, he messed up when Bradford's player–manager Jimmy Scoular chipped a pass into Rovers' penalty area; then he deliberately missed a cross. On each occasion the beneficiary was Bradford's 18-year-old striker Kevin Hector, later to become Derby County's record signing and the Rams' leading goal-scorer and appearance record holder, and, briefly, an England player.

Unfortunately for Million, he never had another opportunity and the game ended 2-2. The *Western Daily Press* summed up his performance:

> Rovers ... did enough to win had goalkeeper Es Million not been in such a nervous mood. Throughout the game he found the slippery ball almost impossible to hold. He was at fault for both Bradford goals and on two more occasions had to be helped out by Joe Davies and Gwyn Jones after further errors had looked like producing more goals.

It was a dreadful day for the goalkeeper. And it was going to become worse. His teammates were angry with him, and the people for whom he was acting wanted their £50 back. Ironically, three days after the match, the Millions' bungalow was sold and their money worries were over. So was his career. In the middle of a training session the following Friday, after the Bristol Rovers captain, Norman Sykes, had gathered the players together, the club's manager, Bert Tann, called them into the boardroom where he accused Million of trying to throw the game. 'Bert knew all the facts. He knew how much I had been offered ... I have never felt so small in my life. I had to admit the allegation was true.'

In fact, Million had made the big mistake of trying to involve his close friend, full-back Gwyn Jones, who refused to cooperate, instead confronting Million during the match: 'Are you trying to throw the game, Es?'

Million was suspended along with Rovers' 26-year-old inside-forward Keith Williams, who had agreed to help, initially for a share of the £50 advance. Williams had been a reluctant match-fixer but his wife was deeply depressed by their money worries – she had attempted to take her own life with an overdose of aspirin – and so he decided to take part. That said, Million would later tell a court that Williams had agreed to participate only if the bribe was increased to £300, which Million was able to negotiate. The suspensions cost Bristol Rovers the services of two players whose total value was £10,000. In reporting them to the League they had put the game of football before their club. Fortunately, they managed to avoid relegation to the Fourth Division by a single point. They finished with forty-one. Bradford Park Avenue totalled forty and went down.

One week after the initial story, on 5 May, *The People* named the go-between. Brian Phillips, Mansfield Town's 31-year-old centre-half, admitted that he had paid Million £50 with the promise of another £250 if Bradford won. Phillips said that he had met Million at Doncaster railway station on the evening before the game at Park Avenue. The syndicate behind the bribe had asked Phillips to approach Million as they had been teammates at Middlesbrough. 'But,' said Phillips, 'the Bristol Rovers players who hadn't gone "bent" played so well that they managed to force a draw.'

Phillips made his confession after playing for Mansfield against Gillingham at Field Mill. Then he drove to the nearby village of Clipstone for a late-night talk with his girlfriend, Pat Leivers, and her parents.

'I'll take my chance with the League,' he told *The People*, 'and if I am kicked out for the good of the game, I hope the syndicate will see I am all right for a bit of cash.'

On the Tuesday after the game, Million had telephoned the Mansfield number that Phillips had given him. A man answered and told the goalkeeper: 'You've lost us a hell of a lot of money. You've got £50 of mine and I want it back. You'd better send it back or you'll be in dead trouble. You know what will happen if you don't.' Million immediately posted his share of the advance – £25 – to 'Mr X' at the Mansfield address given to him. Phillips told *The People* that, so far as he knew, Keith Williams had not returned his share.

On 29 July 1963, Phillips, Million and Williams appeared together at Doncaster Magistrates' Court. Million was fined £100 and ordered to pay £12 10s costs. Phillips and Williams were each fined £50 with £6 5s costs. The chairman of the magistrates said: 'We do not feel that a prison sentence is warranted in view of the defendants' previous characters.' The court heard that Phillips, a former RAF corporal, was now earning £13 a week working as a builder's labourer. Million, whose wife was expecting their second child, was now a bus driver in Middlesbrough on £10 15s a week. Williams, who was married with three children and another one on the way, was also now a labourer, earning £12 a week. Three weeks after the trial, all three were permanently banned from football. Million and his family emigrated to Canada and later returned to Britain. Williams moved to South Africa where set up a business. At 40 years of age, Phillips was too old to resume his playing career when the FA reinstated him in 1971, but he had a successful career as a non-League club manager. Before that, however, he would indeed go to prison.

After the Doncaster trial, Williams told *Daily Herald* journalist Trevor Reynolds:

> Bribery and corruption are rife in top-level football. Police admit they cannot get to the bottom of it and never will. I know that there are 'big boys' behind the syndicate which has soccer under its thumb. They try to fix games all over the country. It's all a question of pinpointing these men and they are all very well shielded

A statement by Brian Phillips named Jimmy Gauld, who Alan Hardaker felt was not telling the truth, as a man who had given him £100 'after the results of certain matches'. Detective Superintendent Joe Smallwood, then head of Nottinghamshire CID, said: 'Our investigations into football bribery are not yet complete. We are still working on the case.'

So was *The People*. Investigative reporter Michael Gabbert, together with one of the newspaper's football writers, Peter Campling, and a small team of freelancers, was on the case too, and, in August 1963, Hartlepool United's Scottish centre-half and captain, Ken Thomson, told the newspaper that in March that year he had agreed to bet with a syndicate on his club losing at Exeter City. He won £200, although claiming that he had fooled the syndicate because he never 'threw' the match: 'I agreed because we had no chance of winning anyway … it was money for jam.'

Thomson, who had been transferred from Middlesbrough (where he had been a teammate of Million and Phillips) for a £4,000 fee the previous season, was probably correct about the Exeter match, which was lost 3-1. That season Hartlepool lost twenty-eight League matches and finished bottom of the Fourth Division, seven points adrift of the next club, Bradford City.

'After that', he said, 'I invested between £50 and £100 with the syndicate. It was obvious to me that the way we kept winning they had other players fixed.'

Thomson was later acquitted of attempting to fix the Exeter game but was found guilty of two other charges relating to Hartlepool matches. One week after his initial confession to *The People* he told the newspaper that it was Brian Phillips who had been his contact with the syndicate. On 2 September 1963, Thomson was banned for life from all football.

For his part in the bribery scandal he would later be imprisoned for six months. He was indeed a sad figure and was only 39 years of age when he died after suffering a heart attack on a golf course in June 1969.

As *The People*'s first major investigation into football bribery drew to a close, the name of Jimmy Gauld was popping up everywhere. Phillips had already said, 'Everything I did was on Gauld's instructions … Gauld was the mastermind behind the betting coups.'

An inside-forward, Gauld had had a long and varied career. Born in Aberdeen in May 1931, before Mansfield Town he had been on the books of his hometown club but had never made the first team at Pittodrie, then he played for Highland League sides Huntly and Elgin City, for Waterford in the League of Ireland, and for Charlton Athletic, Everton, Plymouth Argyle, Swindon Town, St Johnstone and Montreal Cantalia. He was one of soccer's perpetual wanderers, never staying anywhere for more than a season. He had made only four appearances for Mansfield – and scored three goals – before suffering a career-threatening injury.

Gauld's reputation was already tainted. There had been rumours that in April 1960, when he was at Swindon, he had helped fix the result of a 6-1 thrashing by Port Vale, who eventually finished one place higher than Swindon in the Third Division, on the same number points but with a better goal-average (which in those days was determined by dividing the number of goals scored by the number conceded). At the end of that season Tranmere needed at least one point to be sure of avoiding relegation. According to Gauld he was told that some Tranmere players had offered three Mansfield players money to throw the game at Field Mill on 30 April. Mansfield were already safe from the drop. It was suggested to Gauld by a friend who played for Mansfield that if he could get Swindon to lose to Port Vale the same afternoon then 'we could all have a good bet on the two results'. It would be May 1963 before fixed odds betting on two matches only would be banned.

Gauld and two accomplices who were in the Swindon team won on the bet, while the Mansfield trio complained that the Tranmere players had not paid them. Indeed, they were actually out of pocket because one of their Field Mill teammates, the Jamaican winger Lindy Delapenha, had to be paid off after he sniffed out the fix. The rumours regarding the Port Vale game had led the Swindon board to release Gauld but they did not prevent him from finding another club, the Scottish League side

St Johnstone, and then on to Mansfield Town via a summer in Canada's National Soccer League.

In April 1964, Gauld confessed all to *The People*: 'Swindon were comfortably in the middle of the League with nothing to gain or lose, so it didn't seem such a terrible thing to do … but the amount we won was peanuts … But it set me thinking.'

Gauld's thoughts soon turned to organising his own small ring of 'fixers'. And after he broke his leg in a match against Hartlepools United on Boxing Day 1960, a 2-1 win in which he scored, as he waited for the injury to heal and his playing career was in the balance, he developed his betting syndicate and its 'helpers'. He was astonished, he said, at the number of players who wanted to become involved. One of the conditions of taking part was that a player who was going to help fix a result had himself to place a bet on that game. A vested interest. No one was ever paid a one-off flat fee to throw a match, and no one ever knew what other matches were part of the bet that day and thus on what else his stake money depended. Not everyone agreed. When he asked the Oldham Athletic outside-left Colin Whitaker if he thought that the Latics' goalkeeper would be interested in throwing a game, Whitaker replied that he would never consider asking his goalkeeper to do something like that.

Overall, though, between 1961 and 1963 all had gone well for Gauld's enterprise. But he was now under police investigation and in November 1963 he was fined £60 and ordered to pay £10 costs at Rochdale Magistrates' Court under the 1906 Prevention of Corruption Act for six offences of offering bribes to footballers. Banishment from football was not an issue: Gauld's career had ended anyway, although he later received some more legitimate money from the game – £500 from the PFA's insurance fund for those whose playing days had been ended by injury.

Gauld now had another income, however. He began to work for *The People*. He now gathered evidence for Gabbert's and Campling's investigation. Gauld appeared to have no morals. On one occasion he tape-recorded a conversation with his former Mansfield Town teammate Jack Fountain. It was later used to help send Fountain to prison.

On Sunday, 12 April 1964, the pot that had been simmering since 1960 came to the boil when, under the headline 'The Scandal of the Century', *The People* reported on football's 'Day of Infamy – when three Sheffield Wednesday players backed their own side to lose against Ipswich Town'.

The day in question was 1 December 1962 when the only First Division match known for certain to have been rigged by Gauld's syndicate took place at Portman Road. It was a shattering exposure because it involved three such high-profile players – centre-forward David 'Bronco' Layne; centre-half Peter Swan, a former coal miner turned household name; and wing-half Tony Kay, who was now with Everton. Kay had made his full England debut in 1963; Swan had made nineteen consecutive full England appearances; Layne was a regular goal-scorer for the Owls.

Wednesday lost to Ipswich – who were managed by future World Cup-winning manager Alf Ramsey – 2-0 and in a supreme irony *The People* match reporter awarded Kay eight marks out of ten for his performance. In 2013, Ray Crawford, who scored both Ipswich goals that day, told the *East Anglian Daily Times*: 'Tony Kay was the stand-out man-of-the-match, he was that good.'

In the grand scheme of the whole football bribery scandal it did not amount to much. But the status of the players involved did. When most of the others would be forgotten, Kay, Swan and Layne would forever be known as the players who threw a football match. Decades later it is as if the entire 1960s football bribery scandal revolved around that trio because, as *The People* summed up, British football's 'Day of Infamy' had seen 'the ugly cancer of corruption spread its evil growth right up to the highest strata of soccer'.

Gauld had persuaded Layne, a former Swindon Town teammate to become involved. They identified the Owls' game against Ipswich just before Christmas – despite being reigning League champions, the Suffolk club had won only three of their first nineteen League games and were not expected to greatly trouble Wednesday – and Layne then convinced Kay and Swan, who were keen not least because Gauld said that he would cover each player's £50 stake in the event that the bet did not come off. Gauld then arranged for Lincoln City to lose at home to Brentford, and for York City to lose at Oldham Athletic: a nice three-match bet. It worked, but some suspicious bookmakers refused to pay out. Thus, Gauld's winnings were about £1,000 less than he had anticipated, and so the three Wednesday players received only £100 each on top of the £50 stake. Kay told *The People*:

> All I got out of it was £100 and my £50 back, although we were promised a lot more. I didn't reckon right from the start that we had a chance against Ipswich … as it turned out I didn't have to do anything to lose the match – Ipswich got an early goal and that was that.

On the Monday evening following this latest – and most sensational – revelation, Sheffield Wednesday entertained Tottenham Hotspur. At half-time Wednesday's secretary, Eric Taylor, asked supporters to 'bear with the club in this most tragic affair'. Just like Bristol Rovers the previous year, through no fault of the club, Wednesday were about to lose two valuable players. And Everton were about to lose a player for whom they had recently paid a £55,000 transfer fee.

The following Sunday, in more 'shattering disclosures', *The People* named another six players. They were the St Mirren and former Celtic, Portsmouth and Peterborough United goalkeeper Dick Beattie, who was tape-recorded by Gauld and who Michael Gabbert described as 'the worst offender' in the betting ring; Jack Fountain, now with York City and another of Gauld's tape-recorded victims; Halifax Town defender Walter Bingley, another former Swindon teammate of Gauld's; Walsall wing-half Ron Howells, a Welshman who had played alongside Beattie at Portsmouth; Bert Linnecor, a wing-half or inside-forward who had made just seventeen appearances for Birmingham City over a seven-year period at St Andrews and was now coming to the end of a long career with Lincoln City; and Peter Wragg, an inside-forward who was currently the captain of Bradford City.

Bingley, Linnecor and Wragg were not subsequently prosecuted, although serious damage was done to their professional reputations. Indeed, it was impossible to know how many footballers had been involved in fixing matches. The ones named had been randomly ensnared in Gauld's 'investigations' (for which *The People* was reported to have paid him £7,240, a sum worth more than £184,000 in 2024). The rest were holding their breath and hoping to remain anonymous. As was the rule, those who fixed games rarely knew the names of those at other clubs.

On Saturday, 4 May 1964, an FA commission sitting in Sheffield banned Jimmy Gauld permanently from playing football and from taking part in football management. Gauld was not there to hear the verdict in person. For the previous few weeks he had been in Paris, while his wife and children remained at the family home in Berry Hill Road, Mansfield.

The following day, *The People* published his parting words: 'If I could get a year's imprisonment and then have the whole thing forgotten, I would go inside gladly, I wouldn't even ask to see my wife and kids first … I suppose I really decided to go "bent" because of the easy money there was to be made.' His acceptance of a possible prison sentence would not tally with what was later said in court.

Meanwhile, he told the newspaper that one of the disclosures he would make to the head of Sheffield CID, Detective Superintendent William Bowler, was that when match-rigging was at its height, he did not have to recruit players willing to throw matches; they were telephoning him to offer their services. They wanted to 'get in on the act' because the betting ring was winning up to £1,000 every week of the season.

On Monday, 4 May 1964, Gauld was interviewed at the offices of his Nottingham solicitor by Bowler and by Nottingham CID's chief, Detective Superintendent Tom McCullough.

Papers were sent to the Director of Public Prosecutions; two Labour MPs – Roy Mason, the member for Barnsley, and Ellis Smith, who represented Stoke-on-Trent South – asked the Home Secretary to look into the scandal of football bribery; and Alan Hardaker, stung by criticism that, because the Football League could not conduct a worthwhile investigation, the job had been left to a Sunday newspaper, at one stage sought legal advice about banning *The People* from every League ground in the country.

That was never going to happen and *The People* drove on, publishing a story that pep-pills were routinely used by Everton players, and that the Toffees' goalkeeper, Albert Dunlop, had become so addicted to them that he attempted to take his own life. Dunlop also claimed that in the weeks leading up them winning the League championship in 1962–63, a season in which they were unbeaten at Goodison Park, Everton's players had organised a 'bribery kitty' in order to win games. *The People* now equipped Dunlop with a tape-recorder to extract confessions.

At Mansfield Magistrates' Court in September 1964, Gauld and nine other players were committed for trial at Nottinghamshire Assizes in the new year. They went into the dock again in January 1965, where Gauld was described as 'the central figure in the conspiracy … a Judas who betrayed others' and who was now 'a broken man'. All the defendants were found guilty. Gauld's lawyer, Mr E. Appleby, pleaded with the judge not to impose a prison sentence on his client: 'He has had two weeks now in custody in Lincoln prison … He says that prison is dreadful and to him a prison sentence is a terrifying punishment for however long he has to remain there.'

The People's methods had been criticised, but the judge, Mr Justice Lawton, said: 'One of the professional tasks of newspapers is to unmask the rogues and scandals of public life.' He regarded Jimmy Gauld as one of those rogues, ignored the fact that he was 'terrified' of prison, and sentenced him to four years inside, and to pay £5,000 costs.

Passing sentence, the judge said:

> You have done it to put money in your own pocket. You are responsible for the ruin of footballers of the distinction of Kay and Swan. You have ruined the life of an intelligent man like Thomson … I have not forgotten the tens of thousands of people – ordinary citizens – who found relaxation in watching professional football and who, over the period you were operating, paid their shillings to see a match played as they thought by experts … What they got was a dishonest charade.

Brian Phillips and Fountain were each given a fifteen-month prison sentence. Dick Beattie went to gaol for nine months, Ron Howells, Ken Thomson and former Mansfield player Sammy Chapman for six months each, and the 'stars' of the show, Tony Kay, Peter Swan and 'Bronco' Layne each received a four-month sentence. One could not help but think that Esmond Million and Keith Williams had earlier got off lightly with fines of £100 and £50 respectively. Phillips, of course, was now paying the full price.

All the players had been banned for life but when, after seven years, the FA allowed an appeal, some careers, although not all, were resurrected.

Swan, Kay and Layne had kept fit by playing together in the Thorp Arch open prison team – much to the delight of a football-mad governor – and Swan and Layne returned to Hillsborough in 1972, although Layne's comeback was hindered by injury and he ended his career with a few appearances for Hereford United. Swan played another fifteen times, bringing his Wednesday career total to well over 250 games. He later played for Bury and was a successful non-League manager, taking Matlock Town to Wembley in the 1975 FA Trophy Final defeat of Scarborough. He died in January 2021, aged 84, after suffering from Alzheimer's Disease. Except for a few amateur games, Tony Kay did not resume his football career, instead moving to Spain after being accused of selling a counterfeit diamond ring, for which he was fined £400 upon his return to the UK. The bans cost Kay and Swan their chance of being included in England's 1966 World Cup squad.

Dick Beattie's final appearance was for Brechin City in August 1964, while he was on remand awaiting trial. Upon his release from prison he worked in shipyards and died in the village of Old Kilpatrick in West Dunbartonshire in August 1990, aged 53.

After his release, former Northern Ireland international Sammy Chapman played a few games for South African club East Rand United before returning to England where he was allowed to work as coach with Portsmouth and Crewe Alexandra before managing Wolves in two short spells but being unable to prevent them dropping into the Fourth Division after a third successive relegation. Chapman died in Wombourne, Staffordshire, in July 2019, aged 81. Brian Phillips died in March 2012, in Mansfield, aged 80. He had been ill for some time. Ronald Howells was 79 when he died in Bridgnorth in August 2014. Jack Fountain died in his hometown of Leeds in August 2012, aged 80.

Jimmy Gauld, who according to Mr Justice Lawton was 'the spider in the centre of the web', found work as a security guard and caretaker in Marylebone before he died in London in December 2004, aged 73.

Although many of the guilty no doubt went unnamed and unpunished in the 1960s, it is unlikely that this scale of corruption in football continued after such a blinding light had been shone upon it by national newspapers.

Three years before the revelations began to appear, one man, the Real Madrid and Spain star Ferenc Puskas, had the answer to the problem of match-fixing – pay the players more. In October 1960, in a *Daily Herald* interview with journalist Bob Ferrier, Puskas claimed that in English football:

> You make bribery far too easy. How do you think good English players feel about earning less than poorer players in other European countries, and at the same time have to battle through a long championship of forty-two matches? I am not saying that English players are less honourable than, Spanish, French, Italian or Chinese players. People are more or less the same all over the world. But in Spain this kind of thing is not necessary. Even our Second Division players are paid well enough to live comfortably, much better than working people … I think your big clubs earn too much money from football compared with what they give their players … I cannot help thinking that the miserable pay your players get is at the bottom of this whole unhappy business. If a man earns £1,000 for a year's work, as English players do, and someone comes along and offers him £500, half a year's wages, for one mistake on one afternoon of the year, then he has to be a very strong man indeed to resist.

Footballers were not the only people tempted, however. Referees were also the target of the match-fixers …

Chapter 3

A Game of Fine Margins

> We started with Juventus because there were more elements there … almost all the other clubs were involved, let's be honest.
>
> Giovandomenico Lepore,
> Naples general prosecutor

In April 1973, Derby County faced Juventus in the semi-final of the European Cup. Ahead of the first leg in Turin, Brian Clough and his assistant, Peter Taylor, travelled to watch their opponents in a Serie A game. Upon their return Taylor told the Rams' players: 'We daren't tell you what they were like. They played just like a Third Division side.'

Sure enough, the game in Turin began promisingly for the English club. At half-time Derby were level at 1-1. Kevin Hector's goal – the first ever scored by an English club in a European Cup match in Italy – had equalised José Altafini's effort of two minutes earlier.

However, in the second half, Franco Causio, and Altafini again, scored to give Juventus a 3-1 win. And there were some odd goings-on, including a half-time bust-up in the tunnel when Peter Taylor tried to follow the German referee, Gerhard Schulenburg, who was deep in conversation with his fellow countryman, the Juventus player Helmut Haller. Former Wales international John Charles, who was a hugely popular figure in Turin after playing for Juventus, had travelled with Derby as an advisor. He told Taylor that Haller was in the referee's dressing room. Taylor tried to intervene and was arrested, although he was soon released when Charles stepped in.

In the second half, Schulenburg booked both Derby's centre-half Roy McFarland and midfielder Archie Gemmill for trivial offences, which meant that the influential pair would miss the second leg. The situation was not helped when Clough insisted that his post-match words for the Italian press were translated literally: 'I will not speak to cheating bastards. To cheating bastards I will not speak.'

At Derby, the Rams failed to break down a massed Italian defence. Even when Luciano Spinosi tripped Hector, winger Alan Hinton sent the penalty wide. Centre-forward Roger Davies, who had joined the Rams from non-League Worcester City in September 1971 for £12,000, was sent off for reacting wildly to a piece of provocation. The goalless draw put the Rams out.

There were more rumours and the affair was exposed by *Sunday Times* journalist Brian Glanville. Before the second leg at the Baseball Ground, a notorious 'fixer', the 61-year-old Hungarian Dezso Solti, had approached the Portuguese referee, Francisco Marques Lobo, allegedly on behalf of the Juventus club. The referee was offered a car, $5,000 (£12,250), and the promise that Dr Artemio Franchi, president of both Juventus and the Italian football federation (Federazione Italiana Giuoco Calcio or FIGC), would 'promote his career' as an international referee. The honourable Lobo had refused and immediately reported the matter to UEFA who, after hearing the evidence, decided to let him officiate at the Baseball Ground. No action was taken against Juventus or Franchi because no connection between them and Solti could be proved. Franchi was soon to become president of UEFA. And the Derby-Juventus game was the last European match that the honest Lobo would ever referee.

Solti, meanwhile, was banned from football. His story was quite remarkable even before he became a key figure in the business of match-fixing. Born Dezso Steinberger in September 1911, when the Second World War broke out he was working for his father, who owned a mill. In 1944 he was sent to Auschwitz where he survived and worked as a labourer and even kept goal for one of the camp's football teams. He found favour with the notorious SS physician Josef Mengele who conducted inhumane experiments on inmates. Mengele used the Hungarian as a general dogsbody. As Soviet forces neared Auschwitz, Steinberger went on the 'Death Marches', the forced evacuations of concentration camp prisoners in part to keep them from falling into Allied hands and relating their experiences

Steinberger spent time in Dachau concentration camp and he enjoyed several strokes of good fortune before being taken in by advancing US forces. Recruited by the Hungarian secret police as an informant, he then trained as a stage magician, was granted a passport in the name of Dezso

Solti, and in 1949 arrived in Italy in the company of six female dancers who he insisted were essential to his act, but were alleged to be prostitutes being trafficked. His act, Szobel's Show Girls, played at nightclubs in Rome, Milan, Turin and Trieste. He told the International Refugee Organisation that he would be prosecuted if he returned to Hungary and, anyway, he did not want to live under what was now a communist regime. He made no mention of his time spent in Nazi concentration camps.

In Italy, Solti met a fellow Hungarian Jew, Bela Guttmann, who had also survived the Nazi camps. It was Solti's introduction to the world of big-time football. Guttmann, who also left Hungary for Italy in 1949, would become the world's first 'super-star' manager, working with a number of leading clubs, managing the Austrian national team and winning back-to-back European Cups for Benfica.

Solti now worked as a football agent and eventually became enmeshed in the shadier side of the game. In May 1965, for instance, Liverpool lost 3-0 to Inter at San Siro and were convinced that the game – the second leg of a European Cup semi-final tie that the Merseysiders, in their debut season in the competition, led 3-1 after the Anfield match – had been fixed. The first Inter goal came direct from a free-kick that the referee had signalled was indirect; the second after the ball was 'stolen' from goalkeeper Tommy Lawrence as he bounced it.

After the match Liverpool manager Bill Shankly said: 'On the Continent, referees normally protect goalkeepers, particularly in Italy. This Spanish referee did not protect Lawrence. He let Peiro kick him from behind and then boot the ball in while he was bouncing it about.'

Giacinto Facchetti scored a third for Inter, and when Ian St John had the ball in the net for what should have been an aggregate equaliser, his effort was ruled out. St John said later: 'I just remember running through and putting the ball in. I don't know what the infringement was supposed to have been.' Apparently it was for offside.

The referee that evening was the Spaniard José María Ortiz de Mendíbil, who had taken charge of other Inter matches when the Italians did particularly well, not least the previous season's European Cup semi-final when Inter beat Borussia Dortmund 2-0 after drawing 2-2 in Germany. There were some strange decisions that benefited the Italians. Solti's name was always around these controversies.

In his 1983 book *Only The Ball Has A Skin*, the Hungarian journalist Peter Borenich revealed that before the 1966 European Cup semi-final second leg, Solti had offered Hungarian referee György Vadás enough money to buy 'five or six Mercedes' if he helped Inter beat Real Madrid. Vadás refused, the game ended 1-1 and Real, who had won the first leg 1-0 in Madrid, went on to beat Partizan Belgrade in the Final. There was also the story that a Yugoslav referee who somehow managed not to send off an Inter player for kicking an opponent, later enjoyed a holiday on the Adriatic, all expenses paid by Inter.

In March 1990, Solti told film director Bela Szobolits: 'Football is a game of fine margins. All we did was try to ensure those were not against Inter. If a free-kick is going to be given one way or the other, we wanted to make sure we were seen as the victim not the opposition.'

At Inter, Solti had answered directly to Italo Allodi, the club's secretary and, many said, his co-conspirator in match-fixing. After becoming general manager of Juventus, he was accused, along with Solti, of attempting to bribe Lobo before the game at Derby. Solti was suspended sine die but Allodi was exonerated and, indeed, was never found guilty of any charges laid against him. 'He's not corrupt, he's a corruptor,' said Gian Paolo Ormezzano, a leading Turin journalist.

Allodi, the son of a railwayman, was a former journeyman professional footballer who rose to be rich – he had a fine collection of art – and a huge influence in Italian football, both at club and international level. In 2017 he was posthumously inducted into his country's Football Hall of Fame. He had died in June 1999, aged 71, seven years before Juventus was a club at the centre of yet another football scandal that this time threatened the status of Serie A itself.

Derby County, meanwhile, had been embroiled in scandal before – more than once – and they would be again. The Rams had grown from an idea planted by an official of Derbyshire County Cricket Club, and at a stormy annual meeting in February 1890, none other than Derbyshire's Australian Test star Fred 'Demon' Spofforth accused the club's secretary, Samuel Richardson, of embezzling funds. Richardson, assistant secretary of the cricket club and its first captain, was also secretary of Derby County. He admitted that he had been siphoning money from both clubs for several years. With his wife and several of his six daughters – and £1,000 of sporting funds – he fled to Spain, opened a tailor's shop, obtained the patronage of King Alfonso, and lived to the ripe old age of 93.

In the 1930s, Derby signed some of the country's top players, and in the days of a maximum wage for footballers, many wondered how the

Rams had managed to tempt those stars. Although founder members of the Football League in 1888, Derby had never been one of the 'glamorous' clubs; at that time they had never won the First Division or the FA Cup, although they had, very occasionally, come close. In August 1941, a joint FA–Football League commission finally got to the bottom of how the Rams had drawn top names to the Baseball Ground throughout George Jobey's time as manager. Some inventive accounting had seen the maximum wage structure regularly broken and illegal bonuses paid. Jobey was permanently suspended from football (although that was lifted in 1945 and he went on to manage Mansfield Town for a year in the early 1950s), directors were banned sine die, and the club secretary severely censured. The Rams were also fined £500. Five years later, though, they won the FA Cup for the first time.

Derby's scandals were still not over. In March 2009, a jury at Northampton Crown Court was told that following a takeover of Derby County – for just £3 – Jeremy Keith, Murdo Mackay, and Andrew Mackenzie, the club's finance director, had each been paid £125,000 plus VAT by the club, which was not approved by the board. Mackenzie and Mackay were both sentenced to three years in prison, after being found guilty of conspiracy to defraud the club. Keith was sentenced to eighteen months, having been convicted of false accounting. A Monaco-based lawyer, David Lowe, was also jailed, for two years, after being convicted of money laundering. The court heard that Lowe, the legal adviser during the takeover, had received £81,895 for part of Mackenzie's share of the commissions, and channelled it to Mackenzie via one of Lowe's companies registered in the Isle of Man. Keith was also disqualified from being a company director for three years, while Mackenzie and Mackay were both disqualified for five years. The judge, Ian Alexander QC, described the fraud as 'in some ways more reprehensible' than usual. Derby County supporters wouldn't have argued with that.

In 2022, Derby County was relegated from the Championship after the English Football League (EFL) deducted twenty-one points from their final total as a punishment for entering administration and historical financial mismanagement under the ownership of local businessman Mel Morris. The club were found guilty of breaking the EFL's sustainability and profitability rules.

No fine margins this time …

Chapter 4

The Birthday Party

> Bent matches are about not trying, not being in the right place. Perhaps something as simple as taking the pressure off the opposition.
>
> Ken Jones in the *Sunday Mirror*

It was Sunday, 6 June 1971, and in the German state of Hesse some of the most important people in German football, together with journalists, gathered for the fiftieth birthday party of a fruit importer. Horst-Gregorio Canellas was more than just a tradesman, however. He was also the president of the Bundesliga club Offenbach Kickers. And his birthday bash was going to make quite an impact on the game in Germany.

Founded in 1901, Kickers had to wait until 1968 before they took their place in the top flight, although the Bundesliga as we recognise it today had itself been operating for only five years when Kickers joined the elite. They were relegated after only one season, but won promotion straight away. And on the eve of their new season back among the big clubs, Kickers won their first major honour, the 1970 DFB-Pokal (the knockout cup held annually by the German FA, the Deutscher Fussball Bund) with a 2-1 win over FK Köln in the Final at the Niedersachsenstadion in Hanover. The game was delayed until August because the competition was run mostly through the summer after the World Cup finals in Mexico had finished.

Again, Kickers' stay in the top-tier was short and not very sweet. The 1970–71 Bundesliga season had ended the day before Canellas greeted his guests, and after losing 4-2 to FK Köln that afternoon, Kickers were headed back to the second tier, relegated by the narrowest of margins. A single goal in the goal-difference column separated them from Rot-Weiss Oberhausen who were on the same number of points, meaning that Kickers finished next-to-bottom, four points better off than Rot-Weiss Essen who went down with them.

At one stage it seemed that Kickers might escape relegation. Springtime had seen them win four matches and draw four. But they also lost four. Those defeats, and the form of clubs around them in the table, meant that they were unable to pull clear of the drop zone.

Canellas thought that something untoward was going on, but the DFB was ignoring his concerns as merely 'vague suspicions'. So, those gathered for his party – they included the German national coach, Helmut Schön – were about to hear something that they could not ignore. Canellas produced an audio tape which he played to an audience who listened in stunned silence. They heard recordings of telephone calls that Canellas had made in attempts to influence the results of matches for Offenbach Kickers' benefit. He said that he was actually trying to ensnare 'bent' footballers who he suspected of manipulating matches. Those suspicions had been confirmed in early May when he received a telephone call from FK Köln's goalkeeper Manfred Manglitz, who had been in the West Germany squad for the previous year's World Cup finals. Manglitz was heard offering not to 'accidently' let in goals in a game against Rot-Weiss Essen, in return for 25,000 Deutschmarks (worth about £3,000). Canellas paid up and FK Köln won 3-2.

Canellas was not bribing a player to lose a game. He was offering Manglitz money to ensure that the goalkeeper did not 'throw' a match against Kickers' relegation rivals.

When he offered another West Germany international, Bernd Patzke, and Patzke's Hertha Berlin colleague, Tasso Wild, 140,000 Deutschmarks (£16,500) to guarantee a win over Arminia Bielefeld, another club threatened with relegation, Canellas was outraged when Patzke told him that someone representing Bielefeld had already offered 220,000 Deutschmarks (£26,000) to ensure that Bielefeld took both points. Which they did, winning 1-0 in Berlin's Olympic Stadium, with a seventieth-minute goal from Gerd Roggensack who would go on to have a long and varied managerial career, mostly in the lower tiers of German football.

The Bundesliga was only two years old when it had its first taste of scandal. In 1965, several clubs were found to have made payments to players in excess of what the DFB, then still coming to terms with full-time professionalism, allowed. These recordings of various conversations between Canellas and players opened the lid on something much more serious than clubs paying their own players more wages than was permitted.

The DFB investigation that followed Canellas's revelations found that eighteen games that affected relegation from the Bundesliga in 1970–71 had been manipulated and that the staggering sum of one million Deutschmarks had changed hands. Ten out of eighteen Bundesliga clubs were involved, and some sixty players were also named at various stages. Among those suspended for their parts in the affair were Manfred Manglitz and Tasso Wild, who were initially banned for life, and Bernd Patzke who was suspended for ten years. Although those bans were eventually lifted, only Patzke returned to professional football and that was in South Africa's National Football League.

Arminia Bielefeld, who had finished fourteenth in the 1970–71 Bundesliga, two points ahead of Offenbach Kickers, were forcibly relegated by the DFB in 1972 after being awarded zero points for each of their league games irrespective of result. The Gelsenkirchen club FC Schalke was particularly shamed, although the sum of money involved was minor compared to other instances. The DFB's 'chief prosecutor', Hans Kindermann, a judge in his day-to-day role, and a member of the DFB's control committee, found that the April 1971 match between Schalke and Arminia Bielefeld had been thrown – Bielefeld won 1-0 – for 40,000 Deutschmarks (then worth about £4,700) which was apparently delivered in a suitcase to the Schalke players. The Schalke squad included West Germany international Reinhard Libuda, and future internationals Klaus Fischer and Rolf Rüssmann. Fischer had initially received a life ban for his part in the bribery scandal but that was reduced to a one-year league ban and a five-year ban from playing for the national team. That served, he would be best remembered for his 'bicycle-kick' equaliser against France in the 1982 World Cup semi-final.

Maybe the Schalke players then had an attack of remorse, for they went on to lose to both Kickers and to Rot-Weiss Oberhausen. Whatever, when the axe fell they might have avoided heavier punishments had they owned up, but to a man they denied any involvement in the Bielefeld fix. Kindermann pursued them through the criminal court, and in January 1976, eight players received fines ranging from 9,960 Deutschmarks (about £2,000) for Libuda, and 9,000 Deutschmarks (£1,800) for Hans-Juergen Wittkamp who was now with Bundesliga champions and UEFA

Cup holders, Borussia Monchengladbach. Such infamy lives on and fans of some rival clubs still refer to Schalke as 'FC Meineid' – 'FC Perjury'. Ironically, relegated Rot-Weiss Essen was one of the eight clubs who had no involvement in bribery or any other wrong-doing. Maybe that was why they finished bottom of the table.

If Canellas was expecting to be congratulated for his part in uncovering the whole affair, he was to be disappointed. Because he had offered money to Manfred Manglitz, albeit on the face of it to win a game, he was found guilty of 'unsportsmanlike conduct' and was banned for life for holding any office with a German football club. The ban was lifted in 1976, two years after he had retired as the managing director of his fruit import business. In 1977, he was one of the passengers on a flight from Majorca to Frankfurt when it was hijacked by members of the Popular Front for the Liberation of Palestine. The hostages were later freed in the Somalian capital Mogadishu by soldiers from German counter-terrorism. Horst-Gregorio Canellas died in Offenbach in 1999, after a long illness with lung cancer.

In September 1972, DFB press spokesman Wilfred Gerhard summed up the feelings of the organisation. Gerhard, who would later become the general secretary of the DFB, said:

> It has been very much a bad dream. Bribery was always something you heard about in other countries. But surely not in Germany where everyone abided by the rules?
>
> We had to act quickly. There was no point tying to sweep it under the carpet. Football was being threatened. We had to win back the confidence of the public. And the only way to do that was to show them that we were desperate to clean up the mess.
>
> We had to know the full extent of it. We had to cut out the malignancy before it spread. The trouble with this sort of things is that once one has tried it, others will too.
>
> We were astonished by the stupidity of the players. It was almost as if they wanted to be caught. That someone somewhere had to spell it out. And they went along with it.
>
> … The thing we always consider is the effect on the fan. Any suggestion of corruption destroys him. The game becomes unreal. Football can only retain its validity. It cannot be seen as a circus.

Writing in *The People*, Mike Langley said that 'an embarrassing stench of corruption arising from the Fatherland's football' had, after only seven years of existence, seen that 'their national league has apparently gone bent in a big way'.

The 1971 scandal certainly scarred the Bundesliga, and for the next two seasons, average attendances fell from more than 20,000 in 1970–71 to just over 16,000 in 1972–73. West Germany winning the 1974 World Cup reignited interest in domestic football, and the matter was consigned to history – except when 'FC Meineid' played away, of course.

Chapter 5

Nothing to Do With Football

> I came out of the match rather disillusioned and I think our supporters must have felt the same.
>
> Georg Schmidt, team manager of Austria

The El Molinón Stadium in the centre of Gijón is reputedly the oldest professional football ground in Spain. In use since at least 1908, by 1982 it had undergone significant alterations and there was some dispute as to whether it was even on exactly the same site as the original. There is no dispute, however, that when it came to design and sightlines the 45,000-capacity stadium was the worst venue at the 1982 World Cup finals. There is no dispute, either, that it was the stage for one of the most controversial matches in World Cup history.

El Molinón hosted three Group Two matches of España 1982, and they were all quite memorable. On 16 June, West Germany tumbled to a sensational 2-1 defeat by Algeria who became the first African country to beat a European side in a World Cup match.

The West Germans, the 1980 European champions, had been 3/1 to win the World Cup two years later. Algeria were about 1,000/1. The shock result rivalled England's defeat by the USA in 1950, and Italy losing to North Korea in 1966. The Germans dominated most of the match but fell behind to a Rabah Madjet goal after fifty-four minutes. Karl-Heinz Rummenigge equalised fourteen minutes later, but only a minute after that Lakhdar Belloumi put Algeria ahead again. It was their second successive win over West Germany. The first had been a friendly game, though. This time the result was breathtaking. West Germany's manager, Jupp Derwall, shook his head and said: 'It's beyond my understanding.'

The Germans then raised their game dramatically to beat Chile 4-1 with a hat-trick from Rummenigge, despite the fact that the striker was still struggling with a thigh injury and passed a fitness test only an hour before kick-off.

The final group match was between West Germany and Austria on 25 June. On any other occasion, a fiercely fought match might have been expected. On the face it the West Germans had a score to settle: Austria had knocked the reigning champions out of the 1978 World Cup in a 3-2 upset in Córdoba. But previous results in their 1982 group had produced an interesting scenario. Algeria had lost 2-0 to Austria but then beat Chile 3-2 in their final match, which meant that they were now the first African nation to win two games at a World Cup finals.

The immediate significance of their win over Chile, which came the day before the Germans and Austrians met, was that any kind of German victory by one or two goals would see both West Germany and Austria qualify for the next round. There was a range of other possibilities but the final group match kicked-off with both teams knowing exactly what to do in order to benefit both.

Yet whether the result was decided upon before the kick-off is open to question. In the eleventh minute, a linesman kept his flag down when he might have raised it for offside; it was a hairline decision. West Germany's Pierre Littbarski took full advantage and crossed the ball for Horst Hrubesch to clumsily bundle it home. The Hamburger SV striker bent to head the ball but missed and it went into the net off his knee. It was first time in 191 minutes that the Austrian goalkeeper, Friedl Koncilia of the Austria Wein club, had been beaten.

So there was a scoreline that would have seen these European neighbours both proceed to the next stage. Was anyone trying to score again? Well, Wolfgang Dremmler then brought a fine save out of Koncilia, and Paul Breitner missed two good chances for West Germany. Admittedly, Dremmler's effort was not only the second shot on target in the match, it was also the last. Nonetheless, up to half-time there were no obvious signs that the teams had settled for 1-0 to the Germans.

After the interval, however, it was as if it had suddenly dawned on the players that this would do. First Rummenigge played an extraordinarily long back-pass, and then Austria's prolific striker Hans Krankl decided to play the ball back to a defender some 40 yards behind him. There were other isolated incidents which suggested that the players had not colluded. As late as the seventy-seventh minute Hans-Peter Briegel was forced to make a last-ditch intervention when Bernd Krauss burst into penalty area – a goal then would have drawn Austria level and seen West Germany on their way out of the World Cup – but, by then, the crowd had already begun to think that something odd was going on.

The final ten minutes were awful to watch; so bad in fact that Robert Seeger, who was covering the game for an Austrian television station, went so far as to implore viewers to turn off their sets. A German commentator, Eberhard Stanjek of ARD TV, called the display 'disgraceful' and said that it had 'nothing to do with football … you can say what you want, but not every end justifies every means'.

The British commentator Hugh Johns of ITV, who was covering his last World Cup finals, said:

> A few seconds on Bob Valentine's [the Scottish referee in charge of the game] watch between us and going-home time. And what a relief that's going to be. Breitner for Briegel for [Uli] Stielike, names that run off my tongue at the moment and leave a nasty, nasty taste. Stielike … quality players who should all be in the book of referee Bob Valentine for bringing the game into disrepute. This is one of the most disgraceful international matches I've ever seen.

The match ended to a mounting crescendo of boos and whistles, and one German fan demonstrated his feelings by burning his country's flag. Algerian fans, who had originally watched in the hope and no little expectation that they were seeing their country's next opponents, now waved money at the players, and even burned the notes.

So, West Germany 1 Austria 0. And Algeria third in the group table and on the way home, along with Chile who had not managed even one point from their three matches. The Algerians did not go readily, though. Alemi Sekkal, president of the Algerian Football Federation, called for FIFA to disqualify both West Germany and Austria, describing the match as a 'scandalous and immoral act'.

Sekkal said: 'This sinister plot against the Algerian team, carried out before the eyes of the representatives of FIFA … is a grave threat to the noble principles of sporting ethics and an insult to the Spanish public.'

Jupp Derwall rejected the claims that the result had been arranged. 'I consider that a grave and serious insult,' he told the post-match press conference. Hermann Neuberger, the DFB president, was nonplussed:

'The German team had the right to play slowly and safely.' Later, Derwall told journalists: 'We wanted to progress, not play football.' Hans Krankl was happy that 'we made the next round … And I don't give a damn about the Germans.' German substitute Lothar Matthäus added: 'We've gone through. That's all that counts.'

The Spanish newspaper *El Pais* was already angry over Spain's defeat that day by a ten-men Northern Ireland team after the Irish defender Mal Donaghy was sent off in the sixty-first minute. The paper coupled Spain's poor showing with the result of the West Germany match on what it called 'a day of shame'. The newspaper, *Diario As*, accused the Germans and Austrians of fraud, while *Diario 16* said: 'The only thing they failed to do was kiss each other.' The Gijon-based *El Comercio* published the match report in the crime section of the newspaper.

Austrian manager Georg Schmidt admitted it was 'a shameful performance', but said: 'I am not afraid of a FIFA inquiry but I fear it could happen. If it does I will be ready to answer charges.'

Hans Tschak, the head of the Austrian delegation, made an extraordinary statement:

> Naturally today's game was played tactically. But if 10,000 sons of the desert here in the stadium want to trigger a scandal because of this, it just goes to show that they have too few schools. Some sheikh comes out of an oasis, is allowed to get a sniff of World Cup air after 300 years and thinks he's entitled to open his gob.

West Germany's goalkeeper, Toni Schumacher, wrote later that 'there was no formal agreement between the Austrians and us, but we had a kind of tacit understanding'. Schumacher, who in the semi-final against France committed an appalling (and unpunished) foul on Patrick Battiston that left the Frenchman unconscious, joked that his finest save against Austria came as the result of a back-pass from a teammate. He said that he felt ashamed when the crowd booed as the players 'had been more or less strolling around the pitch' in the final quarter of the game.

FIFA spokesman Rene Courte said that it would be difficult to prove Algeria's allegations. 'I don't know whether Austria were tired or whether the Germans would not let them attack more. But when the

Germans saw, and realised, the Austrians were not pressing too much then they decided to assure their qualification, and that's normal.'

After a three-and-a-half hour meeting, Algeria's appeal was rejected. But to ensure that the scenario could never happen again, final group games would henceforth be played simultaneously. The schedule of future World Cups would be arranged in such a way that teams could not know what they had specifically to do in order to qualify from a certain stage.

So Algeria had accomplished something. Lakhdar Belloumi, the man who had scored the winner against West Germany in that sensational opening group match, said: 'Our performances forced FIFA to make that change, and that was even better than a victory. It meant that Algeria left an indelible mark on football history.'

Meanwhile, the West Germany-Austria match entered the annals of World Cup history as 'the Disgrace of Gijón', or Nichtangriffspakt von Gijón (the non-aggression pact of Gijón). For the record, West Germany lost 3-2 to Italy in the Final.

At the FIFA congress on the eve of that Final, Alemi Sekkal again said that his team had been eliminated from the tournament, not by football but by 'extra sportive actions'. It was something which had to be condemned. FIFA denounced the lack of effort by two teams 'in a match', although they did not name either West Germany or Austria. Later, however, Sepp Blatter, FIFA's general secretary, admitted that it was a reference to the West Germany-Austria fixture. FIFA president João Havelange apologised for the performances of the teams and said this must never happen again.

The 'Disgrace of Gijón' was not the first time that two teams decided to call off hostilities to the benefit of both – and we can look back a long way. In April 1898, Stoke City and Burnley engineered a goalless draw to save both their places in the First Division.

They were involved with two other clubs, Newcastle United and Blackburn Rovers, in a series of test matches to decide promotion and relegation between the top two divisions of the Football League. On the morning of the final round of matches, Stoke and Burnley were first and second in a mini-league. A draw would suit them both and the 4,000 spectators who braved strong winds and torrential rain at Stoke's Victoria Ground witnessed a fiasco.

The goalkeepers hardly touched the ball as outfield players passed it to each other – and even to their opponents when their team looked well placed to mount an attack. 'The goal nets were invented for a reason' was one of more gentle remarks aimed at the twenty-two who strolled around the pitch making no effort to cover up their aim. In the second half the crowd tried to stop the game by keeping the football. No less than five were used, and one was sent on to the top of the grandstand. Both linesmen and a policeman tried their best to intercept the ball before it went on to the terraces. Obviously the result was never in doubt and both clubs retained their top-tier status. Newcastle, who had put in a great deal more effort to beat Blackburn, finished third in the mini-league, one point behind Stoke and Burnley. The Burnley goalkeeper, Jack Hillman, had once won a bet that he could keep goal in a charity match with one hand tied behind his back and not concede a goal. How he must have enjoyed that 1898 test match.

As far as anyone knows, the game on that rainy day in the Potteries is the only top-level football match where there was not even one shot at goal. Even West Germany and Austria managed that in Gijon.

Chapter 6

Bribery and Blackmail

> How can you put a price on a European medal? You can take losing fairly but when you know you have been cheated it's desperately unfair and wrong.
>
> Paul Hart, Nottingham Forest player

'Outclassed Forest have no complaints.' That was the headline over the *Derby Evening Telegraph*'s report of neighbouring Nottingham Forest's surprise 3-0 defeat against 'brilliant' Belgian side Anderlecht in Brussels on 25 April 1984. But when the truth was out, the club from the City Ground would have plenty about which to complain.

Forest held a 2-0 lead from the first leg of this UEFA Cup semi-final tie but now they had been 'swept aside by one of the best displays I have ever seen,' according to reporter Kevin Marriott.

It was true that Forest were well below their best. It took the Belgians only eighteen minutes to pull back a goal through Enzo Scifo. On the hour, Anderlecht's Danish international Kenneth Brylle scored from the penalty spot, and with two minutes remaining Edwin Vandenbergh made it 3-0 on the night and 3-2 on aggregate.

Even then Forest might have gone through on the away-goals rule when, in the dying seconds of the match, they had the ball in the net. But Spanish referee Emilio Guruceta Muro – whose appointment had worried the Forest manager Brian Clough, even before a ball was kicked – ruled that Paul Hart, whose header it was that beat goalkeeper Jacky Munaron, had pushed a defender in the build-up. No goal. Justice was done, wrote Marriot. Had Forest gone through, it would have been a 'travesty'. That seemed to sum up Clough's pre-match assessment of Anderlecht as 'the best team in Europe I've seen for years'. But now the Forest boss was troubled by what he had just seen. It had little to do with how good a team Anderlecht was.

After the game there was crowd trouble – this was the 1980s, after all – and police arrested several dozen Anderlecht and Forest fans. Away supporters had been tightly wedged on terraces at one corner of the stadium, and after one surge Forest supporters spilled over into a section of the crowd occupied mostly by Anderlecht followers. Baton-wielding police intervened several times to separate scuffling groups of rival fans, and the ambulance service reported fifty injured, none seriously but another blot of the reputation of travelling British football supporters nonetheless.

Yet during the build-up to the game, Forest fans had been praised for their good behaviour. *Nottingham Evening Post* journalist David Lowe reported; 'Bands of singing, chanting fans soaked up the sunshine in pavement cafes with fans hugging the main square. It was good-humoured and there was no trouble as police maintained a restrained presence.'

As the match itself progressed, however, the atmosphere turned poisonous. Writing in his book *His Way: The Brian Clough Story*, the BBC's Pat Murphy said that he feared a riot and that the Forest manager had helped to defuse the situation by rushing on to the pitch to shake the referee's hand. Wrote Murphy: 'He no doubt wished he could shake his neck instead, but contented himself with a meaningful stare.'

In the press box with Murphy was John Wragg of the *Daily Express*. He said later:

> Clough was particularly angry on the touchline, which was unusual. He was jumping up and down and it was obvious he knew something was going on. This was back in the days when everyone mixed and after the game all the players and officials were together in one big room. Cloughie came up to the various journalists, kissed each of us on the cheek and said, 'Eh, you know we were cheated, don't you?'

Anderlecht would play Tottenham Hotspur in the 1984 UEFA Cup Final (Spurs won on penalties after the two-legged Final had ended 2-2 on aggregate, and there was even worse crowd violence). In the meantime, Forest, who had suffered early eliminations from both the FA Cup and Football League Cup, were left to wrap up their domestic season in which they finished third in the First Division, six points behind champions Liverpool and three behind runners-up Southampton. It had been, overall, a mediocre campaign, at least by the standards set by Clough, who was in his ninth season at the City Ground and could already look back on two European Cup Final triumphs.

But it could have been so different if Anderlecht president Constant Vanden Stock – they named the stadium after him – had not been so desperate for his club to win that he bribed the referee. Or if Emilio Guruceta Muro had not been dishonest enough to accept the equivalent of £18,000. Perhaps the most disquieting aspect of this squalid affair was the allegation that UEFA knew about the bribe some five years before it decided to do anything about it.

In 1997, Anderlecht's then chairman, Roger Vanden Stock, admitted that under his father's chairmanship the club had paid Muro, although it was only a 'loan'. Constant Vanden Stock claimed that an Anderlecht official, Raymond De Deken, who was acting as referee liaison officer, came to him the day after the match to tell him of Muro's alleged financial problems. De Deken said that the chairman had refused time and again, but that eventually the cash was handed to Muro in an envelope. De Deken did not know if the referee had ever paid it back. De Deken was later banned for life by UEFA.

Roger Vanden Stock said:

> He [his father, Constant] refused two, three, four times and in the end, the day after the game, he eventually said, 'All right, I'll give to this man who is in financial trouble, I'll give him a loan of one million francs. In [my father's] eyes this is not bribery but something to help someone. He did not realise the consequences. It cost him a lot of money and it will certainly cost a lot more, certainly. Now everyone will understand why he paid the money.

Another version of events had Constant Vanden Stock approaching a local criminal called Jean Elst. Belgian journalist Frank van Laeken explained: 'Elst contacted a friend in the region, who went to Alicante and spoke to the referee. The referee said, "OK, I'll do it for 1.2 million Belgian francs."'

But there is no honour among thieves, nor indeed among those lurking in the murky surroundings of football bribery. Jean Elst demanded that Constant Vanden Stock paid him for his silence. His associate, Rene Van Aaken, got wind of the bribe and joined in blackmailing Anderlecht.

It transpired later that the Belgian FA had also became aware of the payments to Muro but said that it did not have the powers to investigate the claim, and passed the information – and the buck – on to UEFA, who, according to a BBC *Inside Out* report of 2016, for five years did nothing about the allegation even though it had been aware of the bribery scandal since 1992. UEFA denied receiving the information before taking action against Anderlecht five years later.

It responded:

> UEFA received the dossier in question in 1997 and launched a full investigation led by the then head of the disciplinary department, and the vice-chairman of the UEFA Appeals Body. This detailed investigation included interviews with several persons involved in the case and was the basis of the September 1997 UEFA executive committee decision to impose a one-year ban on Anderlecht. The Belgian club appealed this decision to the Court of Arbitration for Sport in 1998 and since it won this appeal, that meant that UEFA could no longer pursue this case.

Constant Vanden Stock began to pay up, and by 1996, when he stepped down in favour of his son, Jean Elst and René Van Aaken had allegedly received 56 million Belgian francs (about £1.2 million) to keep quiet. After assuming the chairmanship, Roger Vanden Stock refused to pay any more hush money and exposed the blackmailers.

Anderlecht's general manager Michel Verschueren admitted that he also knew about the bribe. Verschueren, who was also in charge in 1984, said: 'This man was acting on his own initiative. He wanted to help the club but we did not order him to do it.' In fact, Verschueren knew Jean Elst very well from a café where they had often played cards together.

At a meeting in Helsinki in September 1997, UEFA imposed a ban on Anderlecht qualifying for a European competition the next time they qualified. In other words, a one-year ban. It was remarkably lenient. Columnist Brian Halford, writing in the *Lincolnshire Echo*, summed up the feelings of most football fans:

> What are we dealing with here? Stealing a sausage from a sea scout camp? No, it's bribing a ref at a top football

> match. Staggering. Cheating is the big issue. Sports most appalling tangent. But what messages is UEFA is sending out here? That would have made clear the risks involved.

What message indeed? Anderlecht appealed to the Court of Arbitration for Sport (TAS) in Lausanne, and in May 1998 the TAS overturned UEFA's decision because it had been pronounced not by the disciplinary committee but by the executive committee which was not competent to rule on the bribery charge. Moreover, UEFA had not respected its own limitation period of ten years. Ironically, Anderlecht had just qualified for the 1998–99 UEFA Cup, and the TAS decision angered Nottingham Forest who had been demanding that they should take Anderlecht's place in the competition.

For their part in the scandal, Jean Elst and René Van Aaken were each jailed for two years by the Correctional Court of Brussels and ordered to pay fines of 100,000 Belgian francs (£2,150) each 'for extortion and attempted extortion of RSCA Anderlecht in the period 1985–1996'. Both appealed the verdict and in October 2001, the Court of Appeal in Brussels acquitted Van Aaken due to insufficient evidence. The prosecution of Elst was dropped but he died in prison. Referee Emilio Guruceta Muro did not live to face prosecution. He was killed in a car crash in 1987, aged 45.

Constant Vanden Stock was himself a decent footballer noted for his speed and heading ability – he once said: 'For anyone who looks closely enough at my forehead they can still see the imprint of the laces where the ball was sewn shut' – whose playing career with Anderlecht had ended prematurely in 1938 due to injury. He managed the Belgium national team from 1958 to 1968.

'Monsieur Constant', as he was known, also managed Belle-Vue Brewery, one of Belgium's biggest breweries, and became chairman of Anderlecht in 1971, assuming the title of honorary president when he handed over to his son twenty-five years later

He had led Anderlecht through a golden era that brought them ten national championships, seven Belgian FA Cups, the UEFA Cup Winners' Cup in 1976 and 1978, the UEFA Cup in 1983 and the UEFA Super Cup in 1976 and 1978. Despite his bribing a referee, Anderlecht never felt it necessary to change the name of their stadium until 2019 when, for sponsorship reasons, it also became known as Lotto Park.

Upon his death in 2008, aged 93, the Belgian FA posted a glowing tribute that did not mention the bribery scandal:

> Firstly, the Royal Belgian Football Association would like to pay its deepest respects to the family regarding their loss. Constant Vanden Stock was an important person in Belgian football, for both the FA and Anderlecht. Belgian football has lost an important figure.

In a public poll Constant Vanden Stock was voted 93rd greatest Belgian of all time. But, so far as Nottingham Forest was concerned, his name was mud.

After the events of 25 April 1984 became public knowledge, Paul Hart, in 1997 now Forest's youth director, said;

> To be honest, we didn't play well that night, but at the time it looked as though we had been cheated out of the game but obviously we were not aware of the full circumstances. I scored what looked to be a perfectly good goal late in the game that would have put us through to the Final. We also had a very, very dubious penalty given against us and the goal that was disallowed was just incredible. He [Muro] said that he awarded a free-kick against me for pushing. I certainly didn't push anybody or anything like that, and neither did anybody else. I scored from a free header. We were all shattered afterwards and I have never seen Brian Clough like that, either before or since. At the airport on the way back, he was absolutely on his knees. This news, I suppose, confirms what we all expected but, to be honest, it makes me feel no better. In fact, I wish I hadn't been told.

In 2016, Nottingham Forest's former striker Gary Birtles told *Notts TV*:

> I was sat on the bench coming back from injury and as a sub, you can see what's happening more than when you're on the pitch. The penalty decision was one of the most ridiculous I've ever seen. We also scored a perfectly good goal in the last minute where there was no infringement but

> it was disallowed; we were off celebrating but they were counter-attacking as a free-kick was given. Brian Clough said he always thought there was something going on, too.

Forest's Ian Bowyer recalled: 'The referee wouldn't even shake our hands. Cloughie came in and effectively told us that the referee was bent and we should just get out of there.'

Clough, of course, had seen it all before, with Derby County in Turin in 1973 when he told a press conference: 'I will not speak to cheating bastards.'

Nottingham Forest initially thought about suing Anderlecht for damages after they had cheated their way into the 1984 UEFA Cup Final at the East Midlands club's expense, but eventually they decided to let the matter rest.

Legal wranglings between the two clubs were not over, however. In March 2023, Anderlecht talked about reporting Nottingham Forest to FIFA over Forest's decision not to let defender Harry Toffolo join the Belgian club on loan, despite the paperwork apparently having been completed. Late in the day, following an injury to another player, Forest needed Toffolo after all. Ironically, he soon found himself with a suspended five-month ban after admitting 375 breaches of the FA's betting rules. Anderlecht had decided not to report Forest. 'That was decent of them,' was the guarded response from Reds' fans still smarting over the events of 1984.

Chapter 7

The Man Who Led a Thousand Lives

> If allegations against the French team are proven then we would ask UEFA to repeat the cup final, this time against Glasgow Rangers. It would be a fair solution.
>
> Silvio Berlusconi, AC Milan president

The general opinion was that the 1993 European Champions League Final between Olympique de Marseilles and AC Milan would be the best since 1962. Thirty-one years earlier, despite Ferenc Puskas scoring a hat-trick for Real Madrid, the Spanish club lost 5-3 to a Eusebio-inspired Benfica in what was then known as the European Cup Final. Now the champions of France and Italy promised another feast of football in the revamped competition.

Writing in the Dublin-based *Sunday World*, veteran sports broadcaster American-born Jimmy Magee, known as 'the Memory Man', said:

> It's the European Final that most football followers would wish to see. Olympique de Marseilles with their collection of French internationals, all on the current World Cup panel, plus the exciting African Footballer of the Year, Abedi Pele, are good enough and classy enough to take the title … A French club has never won the European Champions Cup. Such has been the enormous contribution of France and Frenchmen to the foundation and continued prosperity of world football that a European victory would seem appropriate. The European Cup, the Jules Rimet Trophy, European Footballer of the Year, Golden Boot, Henri Delaunay Cup are all French connections … In terms of big-name footballers it's the most attractive European Cup final since Real Madrid and Benfica crossed horns in

> 1962. There's the potential for more netbusters in Munich. Tactically and technically it should be one of the finest games. I hope we won't be disappointed.

The game in Munich's Olympiastadion did not disappoint the neutral observer – and it delighted those from Marseilles – but, unlike 1962, there was no netbusting feast. The destiny of the trophy was decided by the only goal of the game. Just before half-time, Marseilles's 26-year-old Ivorian international central defender Basile Boli outjumped a crowded penalty area to head home Pele's pinpoint corner. It was enough to defeat AC Milan. Boli had wept after Marseilles lost the 1991 European Cup Final on penalties to Red Star Belgrade in Bari. Now his tears were those of joy.

Before the match, Marseilles president Bernard Tapie had said: 'If Marseilles win the European Cup I might just pack it in right afterwards. It would be such a beautiful chapter in French soccer history.' As it would turn out, the choice would be made for him, although in the aftermath of a famous victory – a French club had never before won the trophy – he vowed to carry on: 'A soccer club takes over people's emotions and brings a special kind of commitment. You just can't drop it like that.'

The Parisian self-made millionaire had taken over the club in 1986 and began buying the players who would take Olympique to hitherto unknown glories. His methods, however, did not sit well with everyone. And there would be a greater price to pay than French francs.

Three days before the Champions League Final, the distinguished football writer Patrick Barclay had given insight into Tapie's style as an interfering club owner. Barclay recalled an incident that had occurred at the team's hotel before a cup-tie in Nantes two years earlier. Tapie was not happy with the club's current coach, the 70-year-old Belgian Raymond Goethals, who had coached a dozen previous clubs as well as the Belgian national team. Goethals had joined Marseilles in January 1991, and in his first season – he succeeded Franz Beckenbauer to become Olympique's third coach of that campaign – he had taken them to the European Cup Final against Red Star Belgrade. Tapie publicly criticised Goethals for falling into a tactical trap set by Red Star's coach Ljupki Petrovic, who admitted that he had played for the penalty 'shootout'. Tapie said that was seeking a coach to help him achieve his European dream, and he approached Liverpool's manager, Kenny Dalglish. Johann Cruyff was also approached but, like Dalglish, declined Tapie's offer.

Goethals survived but still faced Tapie's public ire, in particular because he was not using a 'number-ten', a playmaker to open up angles of attack. In the lounge of the team hotel before the Nantes game, the players were waiting the arrival of the owner, who swept in, 'shaking every hand like the glamorous politician he is', according to Barclay.

Tapie then went into an ante-room, followed by the world-weary Goethals. A few minutes later, the Marseilles team was announced. There was one change: Philippe Vercruysse, a 29-year-old former France international midfielder – 'getting on a bit, but a passer', said Barclay – was in at number-ten. When a reporter praised Goethals on the team's performance since his return as coach, Goethals, who was now in his third short spell with the club after being rehired each time Tapie's other targets did not want the job, smiled and said: 'Oh, I don't know. I'd say that Olympique de Marseilles have had the same coach for six years.'

In some ways, perhaps Goethals and Tapie were not so very different. In 1982, Goethals had been banned from working in Belgium for a year when he was coaching Standard Liege and was found to have helped bribe players from Waterschei, who were Standard's last domestic opponents of the season before the Liege club met Barcelona in the European Cup-winners' Cup Final. Standard won the game 3-1 against an unusually uncompetitive Waterschei, thus lifted the Belgian League title, and had all their players fit to meet Barcelona. Along with Goethals, Standard's chief executive, Roger Petit, and eight senior players – Eric Gerets, Jos Daerden, Walter Meeuws, Theo Poel, Simon Tahamata, Michel Preud'homme, Gerard Plessers and Guy Vandersmissen – were suspended for varying periods.

Patrick Barclay also cited an incident where one of Tapie's dressing-room harangues was interrupted by the Brazilian defender Carlos Mozer. Mozer, who had joined Marseilles in 1989 for a 25 million franc transfer fee from Benfica, invited the owner to discuss the matter in private. Said Barclay: 'Minutes later, they returned, Tapie's tan somewhat diluted as he smoothed the lapels of his blazer. Mozer has left the club.' The 32-year-old defender rejoined Benfica where he managed another seventy-five senior appearances before seeing out his career in Japan.

Tapie, born in 1943, in a rough neighbourhood of Paris, the son of a plumber, was always a man in a hurry. Over the years he was a singer who released several pop songs. He acted in a popular television show. He set up a cycling team anchored by Bernard Hinault and Greg Lemond that won successive Tour de France races. And he held a major stake in the Marseille daily newspaper *La Provence.* He served twice as urban affairs minister in the cabinet of François Mitterrand's left-wing government. His business interests were regularly tainted by controversy – he faced charges of corruption, tax fraud and misuse of corporate assets – and in January 1991, although allegations that Tapie had tried fix league games against Caen, Brest, Saint-Etienne and Bordeaux did not stick, the French football authorities still suspended him for one year for 'damaging sporting morale and insulting referees'. Somehow he managed to remain as Olympique's president and continued to conduct club business

But he also made Olympique de Marseilles the club champions of Europe, and for that the fans were prepared to forgive him almost everything else. And then came the devastating blow that meant Olympique might not be allowed to keep that European champions title.

'European Cup Rematch Call' was the headline. If bribery allegations were proved against Olympique de Marseilles, then AC Milan wanted to meet Rangers, the semi-finalists beaten by Olympique, in a replayed Champions League Final.

The whistle had been blown by Valenciennes defender Jacques Glassmann who claimed that he had been present when two of his teammates, Christophe Robert, who was Valenciennes's captain, and Jorge Burruchaga, a member of Argentina's 1986 World Cup winning squad, had accepted a bribe from Olympique de Marseilles player Jean-Jacques Eydelie – a former teammate of Robert and Burruchaga at Nantes – to 'take it easy' in the forthcoming French league game between their two clubs, even though Valenciennes was facing relegation.

On the eve of the match, Glassmann said later, Robert asked him to help ensure an Olympique victory. Glassmann refused and for that would be awarded a FIFA Fair Play Award in 1995. In the wake of his whistleblowing, however, he was surprisingly reviled by many Valenciennes supporters for his honesty and ended up playing in the French third tier with US Maubeuge.

On 20 May 1993, six days before the Champions League Final, Marseilles strolled to a 1-0 win in Valenciennes, which confirmed their fifth consecutive domestic league title since 1989 – and relegated the home club. The game had been much less physical than normal, and Olympique had no fitness concerns for their next game, the European Final. The goal had come in the twenty-first minute, and two minutes later

Robert was substituted after he was tackled and went down apparently injured, although the challenge had appeared innocuous enough.

Referee Jean-Marie Véniel later said that throughout the game Jorge Burruchaga did not dispute any refereeing decisions, 'which was unusual'. Véniel also noticed that Glassmann had never stopped running. 'Burruchaga usually challenged everything,' he told the French weekly news magazine *L'Éxpress*. 'However, that evening, not only did he not dispute anything, but he asked the others to be silent. Conversely, Jacques Glassmann ran everywhere.'

At half-time, Glassmann told his club coach, Boro Primorac, about the bribe, and at the end of the match police entered the Marseille dressing-room and questioned some of the visiting players. Two weeks later, Christophe Robert contacted a local magistrate and admitted his role in the arrangement to let Marseilles win easily. The whole business was out in the open.

Robert's wife admitted that she had collected the bribe money from Eydelie, and detectives found 250,000 francs (about £30,000) buried in a relative's garden.

On 30 June 1993, police questioned twelve Marseilles players at a pre-season training camp in the Pyrenees. Eydelie admitted handing over the bribe, and he and Jean-Pierre Bernes, Marseilles general manager and Tapie's number-two, were arrested and held in prison on remand. Robert was arrested in the south-western town of Périgueux. His wife, Marie-Christine, was charged with conspiracy.

Le Monde journalists Jérôme Fenoglio and Edwy Plenel broke the story that an unusual brand of envelopes was found during a police raid on Olympique's headquarters and they were identical to the one containing the buried 250,000 francs.

In July a French court ordered Jean-Pierre Bernes to be transferred to Valenciennes where he could be charged by the judge investigating the bribery allegations. Bernes had been detained for questioning after a week of treatment at a Marseilles hospital for exhaustion and depression. He remained in custody in the prison hospital before being moved. The same month a French television crew claimed that they had been attacked by Tapie, who had thrown their cameras into the sea near Toulon.

In August 1993, the man who had lavished millions of dollars on business takeovers and football stars claimed that he was all but bankrupt. Tapie told the weekly magazine *Le Nouvel Observateur*: 'The truth is I am broke.' He said the Paris mansion he bought for 100 million francs (£11.2 million) was partly mortgaged and a slump in the property market had reduced its value to 30 million francs. He had sold part of his antique furniture and a large painting by Reubens. His yacht, *Phocea*, once valued at 50 million francs, was now mortgaged and worth only 20 million. He made no mention of his stake in Olympique de Marseilles. 'I can live with little,' he said.

There followed almost two years of claims and counter-claims – including allegations that Olympique had also tried to fix European Champions League matches against CSKA Moscow and Club Brugge on their way to ultimate victory – before Tapie and the other major figures in the bribery affair appeared in court.

In April 1995, a Marseilles court ruled that Olympique de Marseilles was to be put into receivership as it was no longer able to pay its huge debts. The previous season the 1993 European champions had been relegated to the French second tier because of the match-rigging scandal. Court president Fernand Arnaud said: 'The situation at Olympique de Marseilles who have imminent difficulties such as paying the salaries of their employees, made it necessary to make a rapid decision at the request of the club officials themselves.'

The following month, Tapie was sentenced to two years in prison, with twelve months suspended. It was longer than prosecutors had requested during his trial in March that year when prosecutor Eric de Montgolfier has asked the court to sentence Tapie to eighteen months in prison with twelve suspended. Besides the Olympique affair, Tapie also faced a host of other lawsuits over his collapsed business empire.

A panel of judges had been deliberating since then. They said that the harsher sentence stemmed from Tapie's efforts to conspire with a fellow left-wing politician to produce a false alibi. Jean-Pierre Bernes had claimed that it was Tapie who had ordered him to arrange the bribe – he also said that, over the years, some 6 million francs had been made available to buy the services of opposing players, their coaches, and even referees – while Tapie said that the 250,000 francs at the centre of this affair was merely a loan to Robert to help him open a restaurant.

In fact, both Robert and Burruchaga admitted receiving 250,000 francs each to throw the match. Each was given a 5,000 franc (£625) fine and a six-month suspended sentence, as was Marie-Christine Robert.

Eydelie was given a one-year suspended sentence (he had already served seventeen days) and a 10,000 franc (£1,250) fine. Robert was banned from French football for two seasons, Eydelie for eighteen months. Burruchaga eventually returned to Argentina.

Bernes was given a two-year suspended sentence after testifying that it was indeed Tapie who had dreamed up and organised the match-rigging. Jacques Mellick, a Socialist member of parliament who admitted lying in an attempt to create the false alibi for Tapie, had, that April, been given a six-month suspended sentence for interfering with a witness. An aide to Mellick recanted a statement that they had met with Tapie in Paris on 17 June 1993 at the same time that the Valenciennes coach, Boro Primorac, claimed that Tapie had tried to bribe him to take the blame for the scandal. The aide said that Mellick had ordered her to cover for Tapie.

Meanwhile, Tapie – free pending a possible appeal – criticised the judges: 'They feel that they can do whatever they want. They tried to crush me … they saw I wasn't dead and they started over again … If I set foot in prison I won't get out for ten years.' After an appeal to the Court de Cassation, the supreme court, he would serve only five months inside.

His defence lawyer, Francis Debacker, said that Tapie had not expected such a punishment. He called it 'excessive and unacceptable' as there was no serious evidence against his client. In fact, Tapie's rapid fall from grace was as much due to multiple financial failings as it was to the football scandal. In December 1994 he had been declared bankrupt.

Upon his release from prison, banned from football and politics, Tapie took up acting – he received some rave reviews – and singing, and also continued his controversial business career.

Twice he was convicted of tax fraud; in 1997, when he was sentenced to eighteen months of which twelve months were suspended; and in 2005, when he was sentenced to three years, twenty-eight months of which were suspended. That time he did not return to jail as his sentence was set against the eight months he had already spent in prison. His love affair with Olympique de Marseilles was not yet over, however. In April 2001, he returned to the club as sporting director. 'The hair is glossy, the grin broad, the charm as potent as ever … it was almost as if a rock star had come to town,' wrote *The Economist*. This time, though, it was a short-lived relationship.

Bernard Tapie died, aged 78, on 21 October 2021, four years after being diagnosed with cancer. His death came just days before a French court was due to rule on a long and complex legal battle concerning his selling his majority stake in the Adidas sports company to a group of private investors to avoid any conflict of interests when he was in government in 1993. One year later, Adidas was sold again, this time for more than double the price that Tapie had been paid. Tapie sued the Crédit Lyonnais bank, claiming it had deliberately undervalued the firm. In 2008 he was awarded €403 million (£322.4 million) in damages and interest, to be paid from public funds because the bank was part state-owned. Seven years later an appeal court overruled the award and ordered Tapie to pay back the money with interest. But Tapie said the money had all gone: 'I am ruined. Ruined.'

Remarkably, despite all the guilty verdicts, Tapie had remained a favourite with the French nation. President Emmanuel Macron said that he and his wife, Brigitte, were touched by the news of his death, and that Tapie's ambition, energy and enthusiasm 'were a source of inspiration for generations of French people'. Macron said that Tapie had 'a combativeness that could move mountains and take down the moon … He never gave up.'

France's prime minister, Jean Castex, told journalists: 'The first image that comes to mind is that of the fighter, for his ideas, his convictions. He has always been very committed against the far right, but above all for some causes, for his football team, his city.'

Olympique de Marseilles had returned to the top flight of French football in 1996, backed by Robert Louis-Dreyfus. The CEO of Adidas had seen them re-emerge as a leading European club and the best-supported in France with average attendances of more than 50,000 at their Stade Vélodrome.

A spokesperson for the football club that Tapie had raised from relative obscurity to European fame, but for which he had then been responsible for a rapid fall from grace, said that Olympique had learned 'with deep sadness of the passing of Bernard Tapie. He will leave a great void in the hearts of the Marseillais and will forever remain in the legend of the club.'

As Macron said, Bernard Tapie had 'led a thousand lives'.

Chapter 8

One Hell of a Ride

> Football must be above suspicion of corruption in any form. If it exists it will be ruthlessly rooted out and dealt with. The FA is utterly determined this will happen – and quickly.
>
> Mike Parry, FA spokesman

It was, said the newspapers, the most astonishing fightback of the season. Liverpool, three goals adrift to Premier League champions Manchester United on a damp January evening in 1994, coming back to draw 3-3 with a seventy-ninth-minute equaliser.

Of course, it was all about the goals: Steve Bruce's opening header from Eric Cantona's cross; Ryan Giggs taking advantage of Jamie Redknapp's under-hit back-pass; Denis Irwin's free-kick from the edge of the penalty area. And all within the first twenty-four minutes.

Within a minute, though, Liverpool's revival was under way when Nigel Clough beat Peter Schmeichel with a 30-yarder. Seven minutes from half-time it was Clough again after a mix-up in United's defence. There were eleven minutes remaining when Neil Ruddock's powerful header confirmed a remarkable comeback to leave a near-capacity Anfield attendance of 42,795 weighing up what they had just witnessed.

But if it was the goals that the fans talked about on their way home, when a recording of the match was replayed on a television screen in a darkened room at Winchester Crown Court three years later, jurors were told to focus not on the ball hitting the back of the net, but instead on Liverpool's colourful goalkeeper, Bruce Grobbelaar.

Back in 1994, in their report of the match, the *Liverpool Echo* had described the goalkeeper as 'excellent', picking out 'Grobbelaar's superb stop from the speedy Giggs', a save from Brian McClair that prevented the half-time scoreline from being 'even more incredible', and, the most decisive save of all, 'Grobbelaar's splendid parry of [Roy]

Keane's angled effort'. So why was a jury particularly interested in the goalkeeper's contribution to this amazing revival? It might have helped Liverpool to an unexpected point but what was so special about it?

Bruce Grobbelaar was always in the news. It says as much as anything about his often brilliantly eccentric performances that he bid farewell to his first English club, Crewe Alexandra, by scoring from the penalty spot. He was one of the football's most prominent characters of the 1980s and early '90s.

Born in Durban on 6 October 1957, Grobbelaar made a name for himself in South African football before he signed for Vancouver Whitecaps in the North American Soccer League. The veteran of eleven months' active service in the army during the Rhodesian Bush War might have joined West Bromwich Albion but there were problems in obtaining a work permit. Crewe somehow overcame that, and in December 1979 he joined them on loan. It was Liverpool's chief scout, Tom Saunders, who alerted Anfield, but, his loan spell at Gresty Road over, Grobbelaar had returned to Vancouver. There was, however, a helpful connection. Whitecaps manager, former Blackpool and England goalkeeper Tony Waiters, had once been on the coaching staff at Anfield, and in March 1981, Grobbelaar, now a Zimbabwean international, signed for Liverpool for £250,000, as reserve to Ray Clemence.

The surprise transfer of Clemence to Tottenham Hotspur on the eve of the new season gave Grobbelaar his chance. Along with Mark Lawrenson and Craig Johnston, he made his First Division debut for Liverpool in a 1-0 defeat by Wolves at Molineux in August 1981. He played in every league game that season and was also ever-present for the next four seasons, even though his flamboyant style sometimes led to errors that were particularly unwelcome as Liverpool battled to find consistency.

When the Reds lost 3-1 to Manchester City at Anfield on Boxing Day, the result propelled John Bond's team to the top of the First Division and left Liverpool mid-table. The *Liverpool Echo* reported that Grobbelaar had come in for much criticism, especially when City were awarded a seventy-fourth-minute penalty – he dropped a simple cross and Phil Thompson ended up making a two-handed save – but reminded readers that his brilliant display at Nottingham Forest in the previous game had led to him being named man of the match: 'His problem at the moment seems to be one of consistency.' Liverpool were still in Europe and still in the FA Cup – and by the end of the season, after a remarkable turnaround in fortune, they were Football League champions again.

Grobbelaar would make 628 senior appearances for Liverpool. He was missing only when injured, which was rare, and in 1988–89 when he suffered a bout of meningitis that sidelined him for most of the first half of that season. Grobbelaar went on to win six League championship medals with Liverpool as well as the European Cup, three FA Cups and three Football League Cups. He was the self-described 'most decorated goalkeeper in the League'.

His antics became a feature of his game, not least in the penalty shootout at the end of the 1984 European Cup Final against Roma, when Bruno Conti missed after Grobbelaar started chewing the goal net. Then he wobbled his legs in mock terror as Francesco Graziani stepped up. Graziani also put his penalty over the crossbar and Liverpool won. Grobbelaar also once apprehended a pitch invader and handed him over to police, and there were a few on-field bust-ups with his own teammates as he was never afraid to publicly berate colleagues who he felt had let him down.

That 1993–94 season – Liverpool finished eighth in the First Division after Graeme Souness resigned following a shock FA Cup defeat by Bristol City and was replaced by coach Roy Evans – signalled the end of Grobbelaar's career at Anfield and he was given a free transfer to Southampton. He appeared to be enjoying this extension to his career – he was now 37 – and on 5 November 1994 was involved in a 'cracker of a Bonfire Night game' at Maine Road, another 3-3 draw.

Three days later, as he waited to board an aircraft at Gatwick airport on his way to play for Zimbabwe against Zaire in an African Nations qualifying match, Grobbelaar was confronted by journalists from *The Sun*. They told him that the following day the newspaper would publish a story that accused him of match-fixing. And they had taped evidence of the allegation. Grobbelaar cancelled his seat on the flight to Harare and left the airport, it was thought to consult with his solicitor. He caught a later flight and despite the allegations was cleared to help his country win 2-1, supporters holding placards reading 'Zimbabwe loves Bruce' and 'We love you Bruce'.

By then, of course, the story was international news. At the centre of it was another former Rhodesian Army veteran, one Chris Vincent, now a businessman. After Vincent moved to England in 1989 he and

Grobbelaar become friends, enjoying a full and colourful social life in each other's company. Vincent tempted Grobbelaar to invest £50,000 in a game park in Zimbabwe but the venture failed, leaving Grobbelaar to face a considerable financial loss. Vincent was also in financial trouble and while Grobbelaar still had his annual salary from football (reported to be £160,000), Vincent would be declared bankrupt with debts of £90,000. He needed money, and quickly. In September 1994, he approached *The Sun* with a story that the newspaper could not ignore: Bruce Grobbelaar was involved in fixing football matches – and Vincent could set up a sting operation to trap him.

The Sun provided him with the recording equipment necessary to confirm the allegations. Vincent's first attempt at getting Grobbelaar to damn himself was a failure, but on three subsequent occasions the goalkeeper spoke freely of his attempts to affect the results of matches. The final time was on 3 November 1994, three days before Southampton's 3-3 draw at Maine Road, and six before the story broke.

Five matches were primarily involved. The first was Liverpool's 3-0 defeat at St James's Park in November 1993. Andy Cole scored a hat-trick for Newcastle United that day. Grobbelaar claimed to have been paid £40,000 to throw the game, although none of Cole's goals looked suspicious. Vincent said that after the game Grobbelaar went to the home of Wimbledon's former England international striker John Fashanu who handed over the cash. Fashanu was alleged to be the middle-man between Grobbelaar and Heng Suan Lim, a Malaysian businessman who represented a gambling syndicate involved in match-fixing. Grobbelaar referred to Lim as 'the Short Man'.

The second was the 3-3 draw with Manchester United in January 1994. On tape Grobbelaar told Vincent that he had lost £125,000 by 'accidentally' making two good saves. Vincent claimed that the following month, before a match at Carrow Road, he and Grobbelaar had driven to London to collect £1,500 from Lim. Grobbelaar claimed that he would have picked up £80,000 if Liverpool had lost to Norwich City but twice the Reds came from a goal down to draw 2-2.

Vincent was already secretly filming his conversations with Grobbelaar when the goalkeeper was in the Southampton team that beat Coventry City at Highfield Road on 24 September 1994. Grobbelaar said that he would have made a lot of money had Coventry won 1-0, and after only two minutes Deon Dublin headed the visitors in front. The goalkeeper claimed that he had helped the ball on its way, and the *Birmingham Post*'s Neville Hadsley described Grobbelaar as 'somnolent' in his attempt. 'After that,' said Hadsley, 'Grobbelaar had so little to do, he could have read the morning papers,' as Southampton coasted to a 3-1 win. In the final video, Vincent was pictured giving Grobbelaar £2,000, allegedly as the first of fortnightly retainers until Grobbelaar picked a game to fix, and if that worked out he could expect a 'hundred gees'. Then came the 3-3 draw at Maine Road. Grobbelaar, it was alleged, would have made £50,000 had the outcome been different.

The only question now was: how genuine were these claims of match fixing? Whatever the truth, the football world was shocked – but in some cases initially supportive of Grobbelaar. Southampton's director of football, Lawrie McMenemy, said: 'I can't say a word until I've spoken to Bruce. I won't believe it until I do.' After Grobbelaar denied the allegations, McMenemy said: 'The club will fully support Bruce and there is no question of his suspension or any other disciplinary action while these matters are being investigated.' Grobbelaar played in Southampton's next fifteen league games

Steve Nicol, a close friend of Grobbelaar from his Anfield days, said: 'It's absolute nonsense. There's no way that this is true.' Phil Neal, the Coventry City manager who played for five years with Grobbelaar at Anfield, said that he was 'shocked and gutted' by the allegations: 'I feel very sorry for his wife, Debbie, and their two smashing daughters. There will be a lot of pressure on them. I hope the Football Association investigates as quickly as possible because football does not need this sort of thing dragging on for weeks.'

It did not drag on for too long. On 14 March 1995, Bruce Grobbelaar was arrested as part of the 'Operation Navajo', a Hampshire police investigation into football bribery. He was held at his rented home in Lymington before being taken to Southampton Central police station. There was a surprise new development when 32-year-old John Fashanu, now with Aston Villa but at the end of his playing career after suffering a serious injury at Old Trafford, and Wimbledon's 33-year-old goalkeeper Hans Segers were also arrested. Police said that they had also taken Fashanu's girlfriend, Melissa Kassa-Mapsi, into custody. A fifth arrest saw 29-year-old Heng Suan Lim, the 'Short Man', taken into custody in London.

Of Hans Segers, Wimbledon's assistant manager, Terry Burton, said:

> It's come as a total shock to everyone here. We know no more than you do. We were expecting to see him come in for training this morning. I'm shocked to hear anyone in this country could be involved in this sort of thing, let alone at Wimbledon. Hans has been our number-one goalkeeper for some time and obviously he's played a big part in our success. We'll just have to see wait and see what happens.

In November, Grobbelaar had been charged with misconduct by the FA who now said that they were not planning further action until police had completed their enquiries. The day after Grobbelaar was charged by the FA, Fashanu had claimed that attempts were being made to 'stitch me up'. 'Attempts to involve me in the allegations surrounding Bruce were the last straw that broke the camel's back.'

On Sunday, 12 January 1997, Bruce Grobbelaar, who was now on Plymouth Argyle's books, helped Zimbabwe to a 3-0 victory over Togo in a World Cup qualifying match in the National Sports Stadium in Harare. Two days later he was in the dock at Winchester Crown Court accused of attempting to fix football matches for cash. Alongside him were fellow footballers John Fashanu and Hans Segers, and the 'Short Man', Heng Sun Lim. All four pleaded not guilty. They were all charged under Section 1 (1) of the 1906 Prevention of Corruption Act. Charges against Melissa Kassa-Mapsi, who was now Mrs John Fashanu (the couple had married shortly after the story broke in 1995), had been dropped.

Prosecutor David Calvert-Smith told the court: 'The Crown alleges that Mr Sim was the representative of a syndicate here and actually made some of the early payments to Mr Grobbelaar.' He said that the money was paid to Grobbelaar, while he was a goalkeeper with Liverpool and Southampton, and to Segers who was with Wimbledon. In return they agreed to influence the results of matches. Calvert-Smith said that Fashanu also received large sums of money that could not be explained by his wages from football.

Grobbelaar denied accepting £40,000 from Fashanu for influencing the result of the Newcastle United v Liverpool match in November 1993, and he also denied accepting £2,000 from Chris Vincent for influencing the outcome of an unspecified match in 1994. Segers denied accepting £19,000 from Fashanu for fixing a football match or matches. Fashanu denied paying Grobbelaar, £40,000 and paying cash to Segers.

Their trial would last for thirty-four days, during which the jury would be treated to a raft of claims and counter-claims, and plenty of video recordings of football matches in Court Three at Winchester, the same courtroom in which serial-killer Rosemary West had been tried fifteen months earlier.

Grobbelaar's defence was straightforward and simple: he had accepted Chris Vincent's invitation to discuss fixing football matches only in order to gather evidence to take to the police. He said that he went along with it in the hope of discovering the identities of those behind the plot to influence the outcome of matches. Yes, he had discussed throwing games but it was part of his plan to learn who was behind the match-rigging business.

As for Heng Suan Lim, he had only ever advised him on football matches, provided forecasts. He had never agreed to throw a game for him or anyone else. In fact, said Grobbelaar, he had previously been paid for forecasting in a Norwegian newspaper and on a South African radio station. At no time had he ever forecast results for Liverpool, his club for thirteen years. When Fashanu introduced him to Lim he was to be paid £250 a week if his predictions proved accurate. He had no idea whether or not Lim was placing bets.

David Calvert-Smith, who in October 1998 would become Director of Public Prosecutions and head of the Crown Prosecution Service, insisted that there was a significant difference between being paid for a newspaper column or a radio programme, and accepting money from Lim. 'What I am suggesting is that it is a rather sly way in which you got involved.' Grobbelaar replied: 'It's not much different from what I have been doing … I was never hooked. I did not think it was sly.'

Grobbelaar's barrister, Rodney Klevan QC, played extracts from several games featuring the goalkeeper, and asked for the jury to see the full ninety minutes of the 3-3 draw with Manchester United. The game was shown on three television sets with the judge, Mr Justice Tuckey, together with jury members and counsels, listening on headphones. In the video of his conversation with Vincent about Liverpool's 3-0 defeat at Newcastle in 1993, Grobbelaar said: 'I knew I could do big business there ... they had big bucks so I got the cash.' Again, Grobbelaar told the court, he was just stringing Vincent along.

The jury watched no less than sixteen video extracts from games in which Hans Segers had played. They included footage from Wimbledon's 3-2 defeat by Everton at Goodson Park in the final game of the 1993–94 season. Everton's eighty-first-minute winning goal was enough to keep them in the Premier League.

Segers had dived to his right but could not keep out Graham Stuart's shot. Asked about the state of the pitch, the goalkeeper described it as 'quite rough, there's bits and bobs'.

The recording of the goal was replayed in slow motion, and Segers said: 'I had it covered with my right hand and, just before it bounced in front of me, it hit something, changed direction and just popped up. There was no way I could have saved it ... if we had won they [Wimbledon FC] promised us a trip to America.' Asked if he had made any effort to lose the match, he replied, 'No way.'

Explaining why he and John Fashanu spoke so often by mobile phone, Segers said that the two were both 'playing away' and had an arrangement to cover for each other. The prosecution had claimed that the calls were further evidence of a match-fixing arrangement. Segers's defence barrister, Desmond Da Silva QC, asked him: 'Did you always – to coin a phrase – play at home?'

'I played a few away matches,' Segers said, and he also 'did a few favours' for Fashanu: 'He was covering up for me. I would say if my wife calls, you say I was with you.' Eventually, Segers's wife, Astrid, told him that 'if anything like this happened again I would be packing my suitcase'. Mr Da Silva asked: 'She showed you a yellow card?' 'Yes,' said Segers, 'I was booked.'

Segers admitted depositing £104,000 into a Swiss bank account to avoid paying income tax. The prosecution claimed that the money came from a Far East betting syndicate. Segers, who had previously played for the Dutch club PSV Eindhoven, said that Lim had paid him £1,500 a time simply to forecast the results of matches.

And so it went on – some 12,000 pages of police evidence and at a cost estimated to be £10 million – for thirty-four days until, on Tuesday, 5 March 1997, a halt was called. The jury of eight men and three women – the twelfth member had stood down earlier in the trial – had retired to at 11.05am the previous day to consider their verdict, and in the mid-afternoon Justice Tuckey had told them that he would accept a 10-1 majority verdict. Eventually, after one minute short of eleven hours, the jury concluded that they could not reach a verdict on any of the defendants on any count. The judge said that there were two options: ask the jury to return the following day; call a halt to the trial there and then.

At 4.04pm the jury was summoned back to Court Three. The clerk asked the foreman: 'Have you reached a verdict on any defendant on any count on which at least ten of you are agreed?'

'No,' the foreman replied.

Justice Tuckey: 'I don't want you to say how you are divided, but, obviously you are divided … Could you please tell me if there is any reasonable chance tomorrow of you reaching any verdict in this case in which of at least then of you are agreed?'

Foreman: 'I don't believe so, my lord. We don't believe so.'

Justice Tuckey: 'You have obviously had time to reflect on that answer?'

Foreman: 'We have my lord.'

Justice Tuckey: 'I think that's it. I don't think it's legitimate for me to go beyond that answer and I'm sure it has been carefully considered and in those circumstances, I have no alternative but to discharge the jury from giving a verdict.'

David Calvert-Smith said that the normal procedure was for the case to be retried: 'That is the intention of the Crown and I will be taking instructions at the highest level.'

Justice Tuckey later told the ten barristers involved in the case that any retrial would have a new judge: 'I'm not making any football jokes but there will be a substitute.'

Outside the court a 'disappointed' Bruce Grobbelaar was also in a joking mood: 'We could try a penalty shoot-out.' His solicitor, David Hewitt, said: 'We had hoped for a positive result but it was not to be. Bruce maintains his innocence as he has done throughout. The one thing that has emerged during this trial is that Bruce has never thrown or attempted to throw a football match in his life.' As he walked away with his wife Debbie, Grobbelaar called to waiting journalists and television crews: 'See you next time.'

Segers's solicitor, Mel Goldberg, told reporters: 'We're all very disappointed. It is unsatisfactory for the Crown, the defendants and lawyers. But we are still confident of an acquittal … I was tempted to bash the jurors' heads together.'

Fashanu's solicitor, Henri Brandman, said that they would be making no comment on the outcome.

When asked if maintained his innocence, Heng Suan Lim replied: 'Yes, absolutely no doubt. I always have and I will continue to do so. If they want us to go through it again, we have to wait for that announcement.'

And they did want them to go through it again, although criminal lawyer Gavin Millar, a spokesman for the Bar Council, told the *Daily Mirror*:

> The prosecutions difficulty is that they have to prove the case beyond reasonable doubt. A hung jury is a pretty clear indication that they haven't got the case to do that. If there are three, four or five members of a jury who are saying "No," then you haven't got a clear-cut case. And, statistically, there must be less chance of getting a conviction the second time around.

Three months later, however, a retrial began. On Wednesday, 4 June 1997, in the same Winchester courtroom as before but with a different judge, this time Mr Justice McCullough, it began over again with a Crown Prosecution spokesman saying, 'We're making no estimate,' when it came to how long proceedings would last. The prosecutor would again be David Calvert-Smith, who was now a QC.

More than 100 witnesses would be called, including several well-known former footballers, among them Gordon Banks, England's goalkeeper in the 1966 World Cup triumph. Banks would tell the court that he had watched videos of matches between Newcastle United and Liverpool, Liverpool and Manchester United, Norwich City and Liverpool, Coventry City and Southampton, and Manchester City and Southampton – and that there was 'not a scrap of evidence' in any of them that Bruce Grobbelaar had acted improperly.

Former Arsenal goalkeeper Bob Wilson, now a broadcaster, also watched videos of games in question, and had nothing but praise for the players involved. After the trial, Wilson said that anyone choosing a goalkeeper to throw a match would be wasting their money: 'I wouldn't pick a goalkeeper; it's too obvious.'

Finally, after a nine-week trial, another eleven-person jury deliberated for twenty-six hours spread over five days before finding the four defendants not guilty of all charges, except that they could reach a verdict on the charge of Grobbelaar corruptly accepting £2,000 from Chris Vincent. Grobbelaar had to wait an extra day before the prosecution withdrew that charge.

Surprisingly, the betting industry also agreed that stories of betting syndicates bribing players to fix matches was hard to a accept. A spokesman for William Hill said: 'We are not a charitable cause. We don't want to put ourselves on the firing line to be taken for a ride.'

The Crown Prosecution Service did not push for an appeal against the verdicts but defended its decision to proceed for a second time: 'We are all satisfied that this prosecution was properly brought by the CPS.'

Chris Vincent had apparently been paid £33,000 by *The Sun*, and he now admitted that he stood to make £100,000 from a book about the scandal, although that seemed to have been dependant on guilty verdicts. Grobbelaar's QC, Rodney Klevan, accused Vincent of turning on his former business partner and friend 'like a viper'. 'Correct sir,' Vincent replied.

Buoyed by the not guilty verdict, Grobbelaar decided to sue *The Sun* for libel. In July 1999, the High Court awarded him £85,000 in damages. *The Sun* appealed the verdict, and the Court of Appeal overturned the lower court's decision on the grounds that it was 'perverse'. Lord Justice Simon Brown found Grobbelaar's explanation 'quite incredible', and the High Court's decision was 'a miscarriage of justice that this court must correct'.

Still the affair was not quite over. In October 2002, a majority of the Law Lords ruled that Grobbelaar had indeed been libelled over match-fixing claims – but because he had acted in a 'corrupt manner' they awarded him only £1 in damages.

Lord Bingham said:

> Until 9 November 1994 when the newspaper published its first articles about him, the appellant's public reputation was unblemished. But he had in fact acted in a way in which no decent or honest footballer would act and in a way which could, if not exposed and stamped on, undermine the integrity of a game which earns the loyalty and support

> of millions … It would be an affront to justice if a court of law were to award substantial damages to a man shown to have acted in such flagrant breach of his legal and moral obligations.

Grobbelaar was also ordered to pay *The Sun's* legal costs, estimated at £500,000. He had already run up considerable legal costs of his own, and he was declared bankrupt in England. He said: 'The Britons bankrupted me. I came to their country with £10 in my pocket, and they gave me £1 back. But, in between, I had one hell of a ride.'

Chapter 9

Red Card for the Ref

> Bent referees are vampires of our worst imaginings and all the more scary for being always unproven.
>
> Mike Langley, *Daily Mirror*

It was a difficult time in the affairs of Grasshoppers. On 16 October 1996, a forty-second-minute goal by Auxerre's Thomas Deniaud had put the Swiss club's chances of reaching the knockout stage of the European Champions League in jeopardy.

The result at Auxerre's Stade Abbé-Deschamps was something of a surprise. In their first two Group A matches, Grasshoppers had beaten Rangers 3-0 at the Stadion Hardturm in Zurich, and Ajax 1-0 in Amsterdam, while Auxerre had lost 1-0 at home to Ajax before winning 2-1 at Ibrox.

But there was help at hand. Although not the kind of help that any honest football club would accept. Two days after their defeat by Auxerre, Grasshoppers' general manager, Erich Vogel, was in his office when he received a visit from Kurt Röthlisberger, a Swiss referee. Röthlisberger was a well-known figure in European football. He had taken charge of the 1993 Champions League Final between Olympique de Marseilles and AC Milan. Less auspiciously, he had been sent home from the 1994 World Cup finals in the United States after admitting he had missed an obvious penalty when Germany's Thomas Helmer chopped down Belgium's Josip Weber from behind at Soldier Field in Chicago. The score was 3-1, and so a penalty for Belgium and a red card for Helmer would have given hope to the Belgians: they would have been only a goal down, assuming the penalty was converted, and now playing against ten men. But there was no spot-kick and Helmer remained on the pitch.

Belgium did manage to score again from open play, but, thanks to Röthlisberger's blunder, a full-strength Germany won 3-2 and went into the quarter-finals. There was no VAR in 1994. Ironically, Röthlisberger owned up to his mistake after watching a video recording.

Under under the headline 'Red card for the referee', the Walloon daily newspaper *La Derniere Heure* commented: 'Switzerland was famous for its banks and its chocolate. Now, she will also be famous due to a certain Kurt Röthlisberger, international referee, who distinguished himself on Saturday by refusing [Belgium] a penalty for an unmistakable foul by Helmer on Josip Weber.'

FIFA General Secretary, Sepp Blatter, said. 'He admitted that he made a mistake. He knows that's it for him.' Blatter's willingness to openly criticise referees – FIFA also sent home Italy's Pierluigi Pairetto, Arturo Brizio of Mexico and Jamal Al-Sharif of Syria – was not popular with everyone. Vincent Mauro of the US Soccer Federation, who was a referee at the 1990 World Cup finals, said: 'It surprised a lot of people … I think that FIFA is trying to send a message.'

Former World Cup referee George Courtney, from Spennymoor in County Durham, agreed. 'I couldn't believe it when I heard that FIFA had sent home one of the world's best referees. I was taught that the referee's decision is final, but now it doesn't seem the case.'

Manchester United supporters had also wanted to send a message to Kurt Röthlisberger after he red-carded Eric Cantona at the end of a Champions League second-round second-leg match against Galatasaray at the Ali Sami Yen stadium in Istanbul in November 1993. Röthlisberger had shown Cantona the card when the Frenchman apparently told the referee what he thought of his performance (some witnesses said it was gestures, not words, that offended the referee). On a night of brutal football on the pitch and terrifying behaviour by home supporters – and local police – off it, the goalless draw saw United eliminated on the away-goals rule after a 3-3 draw at Old Trafford. Cantona, who was also on the wrong end of a Turkish policeman's truncheon, was convinced that Röthlisberger had been bribed. He told the French daily sports newspaper *L'Equipe*: 'I am certain referees have been bought in the European Cup and I ask myself whether Mr Röthlisberger had not also been bought.' The Wimbledon FC owner, Sam Hamman, weighed in with his view: 'Surely no sane person can believe that Mr Cantona actually believes that the referee was actually bribed and cheated.'

In 2011 a former Turkish referee and sports commentator, the perfectly sane Ahmet Cakar, claimed that Galatasaray had indeed bribed

Röthlisberger to fix the result. By then, thanks to Grasshoppers' Erich Vogel, everyone knew that this former schoolteacher – Röthlisberger spoke no less than eleven languages, including French which was probably why he could fully appreciate Eric Cantona's views, or at least his Gallic sign language, as the players left the field in Istanbul – was indeed up for taking a payment in return for arranging the manipulation of football matches.

Röthlisberger's visit to Vogel's office in the wake of that disappointing result against Auxerre was not simply to commiserate. He also had a suggestion that might help Grasshoppers on their way into the quarter-finals of the Champions League.

Despite Röthlisberger being Swiss, Vogel, general manager of a Swiss club, did not know him personally, so he was surprised by the visit. Vogel was even more surprised when Röthlisberger said that the referee for the home match against Auxerre, Vadim Zhuk of Belarus, was a friend of his. And for a fee, he could be persuaded to be 'positive for Grasshoppers, negative for Auxerre'.

Vogel told the distinguished *Daily Mirror* and *Sunday Mirror* journalist Mike Langley:

> In thirty-three years of football I've never come across anything like this. Match-fixing, even if you wanted to try it, is both very difficult and very dangerous. So I was astonished. At first Röthlisberger admitted to UEFA that everything I said was correct. Later he told a newspaper that he was only trying to see if Erich Vogel was corrupt or not.

According to Mike Langley the payment that Röthlisberger suggested was 100,000 Swiss francs (£40,000). As Langley wrote, Vogel had two options: reach for the cheque book; reach for the telephone. He chose the latter, and in March 1997, UEFA imposed a lifetime ban on Röthlisberger for attempted bribery.

A UEFA statement said: 'Mr Röthlisberger asked whether the Grasshoppers club would be interested in the referee of the Grasshoppers club v Auxerre match on 30 October 1996 not giving decisions against Grasshoppers. This would obviously involve financial compensation … Mr Röthlisberger said he was friendly with the referee and that it would be easy to arrange the matter.'

Vadim Zhuk, who remained in charge when Grasshoppers beat Auxerre 3-1 in the return match at the Stadion Hardturm, was taken off FIFA duty while investigations continued after the March 1997 hearing. Nothing was found to suggest that Zhuk would have accepted a bribe. He had FIFA's trust and in the summer of that year he went on to referee World Cup qualifiers between Finland and Norway, and between Macedonia and Iceland. Despite beating Auxerre second time around, Grasshoppers lost their final two group matches, 2-1 away at Rangers and 1-0 at home to Ajax, and so did not qualify.

Röthlisberger, meanwhile, unsuccessfully appealed his lifetime ban. Retired English referee Philip Don, who became head of refereeing at the FA towards the end of the 1990s, remembered Röthlisberger as a man who might have refereed the 1994 World Cup Final but for his howler in the Germany-Belgium match. Don told Mike Langley that Röthlisberger was 'a typical teacher'. 'Very conscientious as a ref, honest, and, at one stage, probably under consideration for the Final. Röthlisberger and Sandor Puhl were the most experienced among us in Dallas [the referees' base for the competition]. I thought it was between those two.' It was the Hungarian Puhl who took the World Cup Final between Brazil and Italy in the Rose Bowl, Pasadena.

Jack Taylor, the English referee from Wolverhampton who took the 1974 World Cup Final, told Langley: 'Things can be misconstrued. If a game doesn't go your way, it doesn't mean the ref is involved. In fact, I don't think there's any corruption at all. I see today's refs as hardworking, very good in a game that's getting more difficult.'

Langley pointed out: 'I would love to believe Jack Taylor and, indeed, I do think he's 99 per cent right. But when billions slosh around the world game these days, it's naive to imagine that nobody will try to pour some into a referee's pocket.'

Chapter 10

Lights Out!

> Maybe every stadium in the Premier League should have a generator to make sure there is enough electricity. You cannot accept that every time people turn on their Christmas trees you cannot play a football match.
>
> Arsène Wenger

It seemed an unusual question, but on Monday, 16 August 1999, each member of a jury of nine men and three women preparing to sit on a case at Middlesex Guildhall Crown Court was asked whether they supported either Charlton Athletic or Liverpool.

A juror's favourite football team rarely concerns the courts, but here it was most relevant to ensure that justice could not only be done but really could be seen to be done in the case of a self-styled professional gambler, 38-year-old Hong Kong-born Wai Yuen Liu, who had pleaded not guilty to a charge of conspiracy to cause a public nuisance in February that year.

The story went back much further than that, however. Almost two years, to 3 November 1997 at Upton Park, the home of West Ham United who, that misty Monday evening, were entertaining relegation-threatened fellow Londoners Crystal Palace. Palace had taken a surprise two-goal half-time lead through Neil Shipperley. Seven minutes into the second half, John Hartson pulled back a goal for West Ham, and in the sixty-fifth-minute Frank Lampard equalised. Lampard's teammates were still congratulating him when the floodlights went out. Half an hour later, with no sign of them coming on again, referee David Elleray abandoned the game and 23,778 disappointed football fans made their home.

West Ham's managing director, Peter Storrie, explained to journalists: 'The floodlights at the south end contracted a fault. As this end controls the floodlights for both ends of the ground, that is why the whole system went down.' The following day the *Daily Mirror* ran the headline: 'Regrets, I've had a fuse (but then again, 2-2 is worth a mention).' The newspaper's Tony Stenson felt that it was 'a shame that all the hard work and drama was in vain'. Indeed it was, because up to that point the fans had been treated to some entertaining football with no indication of what the result might be.

On Monday, 22 December, it happened again, this time at Selhurst Park to where Wimbledon had decamped from their old Plough Lane ground. After a goalless first half against Arsenal, the second period was only fifteen seconds old when the floodlights failed. After a fifteen-minute delay the fault was apparently repaired, but as soon as the teams reappeared the lights failed again and the match was abandoned. Arsenal manager Arsène Wenger was understanding but cross: 'It's not Wimbledon's fault, but it's not the first time that it's happened this season and the Premier League must find a solution.'

The Dons' chairman, an embarrassed Sam Hammam, agreed: 'The Premier League chairmen are having an informal meeting in the new year and this should be the first point on the agenda … the dignity of the entire Premier League is at stake here and something should be done to make sure it doesn't happen again. There is so much money in the game these days that it is not beyond the League to make sure that there is some sort of backup system in place. It's the fourth time it's happened to us this season. As well as tonight and at Derby, we've had problems with reserve games at Southampton and Chelsea. It seems to be happening everywhere.'

Floodlight failures in football have always been rare, but there had already been at least one other such incident in the Premier League at the very start of that 1997–98 season, and poor Wimbledon were involved in that too. On Wednesday, 13 August, the Dons were the visitors for the first-ever Premier League game at Derby County's new Pride Park's stadium. Eleven minutes into the second half, with Derby winning 2-1, the floodlights failed. In fact, all the lights went out and the stands were switched to emergency lighting to enable supporters to go about safely. After a delay of more than half an hour, while engineers tried unsuccessfully to restart two failed generators, the referee, Uriah Rennie, abandoned the match. Derby's vice-chairman, Peter Gadsby, said: 'We had eleven maintenance people on duty including six electricians but nobody has yet worked out why both generators failed. There was a bang of such strength that it fused them both.' Then games at Upton Park and at Selhurst Park suffered the same fate. While one such event might be accidental, three might be more than a coincidence. Ultimately, the incident at Pride Park was deemed to be simply an accidental power failure. It was conjectured that the Derby power-cut, a genuine accident though it was, might have provided the inspiration for those that followed. There was, however, quite a time gap between the subsequent floodlight failures of 1997–98 and what happened next.

On 10 February 1999, three days before an evening Premier League match between Charlton Athletic and Liverpool, police arrested three men at The Valley, home of Charlton. The trio were apprehended as they made their way to plant an electrical circuit-breaker which was to be triggered by remote control when the score during the visit of Liverpool favoured a betting syndicate. Because it was all to do with gambling. If British football matches were abandoned at half-time, then betting rules in the Far East meant that the score stood. Graham Sharp, a spokesman for bookmakers William Hill, explained: 'Domestically all bets are void if the match is abandoned. You keep your stake money but it's impossible to make any money. In the Far East the result stands.'

On the eve of the Charlton-Liverpool game, the three men, Wai Yuen Liu (38), Chee Kew Ong (49) and Eng Fwa Lim (35), appeared before Horseferry Road Magistrates' Court. Police had found enough electrical equipment in a car and in a hotel room both connected to the group to sabotage a further eight football matches. Hong Kong born-Liu denied the charge of conspiracy to cause a public nuisance. Malaysians Lim – who was an electrical engineer from Penang – and Ong admitted the same charge. They were sent for trial at Crown Court.

Two months before the attempted sabotage, Ong and Lim had visited The Valley posing as the managers of a new stadium in the Far East. But how had the men gained access to Charlton's ground a few days before the Liverpool match? They had promised to pay 49-year-old security guard Roger Firth £20,000 to give them access to the stadium in order to plant a device. Firth had rashly attempted to bribe a fellow security guard with £5,000 in return for him turning a blind eye when the electrics were being worked on. The police were tipped off. On 10 February,

Firth unlocked the ground and the plant room in order to let the three men inside to set up the device. The trio, unaware that they were being watched, pulled up in Liu's BMW and were arrested. Firth was arrested as he walked home.

Firth said later that Ong had boasted to him that the team had sabotaged two previous games, between West Ham United and Crystal Palace in November 1997, and between Wimbledon and Arsenal that was blacked-out a month later. Those matches had apparently netted organised crime gangs in the Far East up to £60 million.

The gambling ring centred on the fact that betting on Premier League football matches was hugely popular in Malaysia where there had been major corruption in the domestic game; in the mid-1990s, more than 100 players, coaches and referees had been arrested there for attempts to fix matches. An investigation by Malaysian police had led to many leading players being banned, and fans had instead turned their attention to the Premier League football being screened by Sky TV. Top English clubs like Liverpool, Manchester United and Arsenal now had fanatical followings in the Far East where hundreds of syndicates controlled an illegal betting industry in which as much as £30 million could ride on the outcome of a single game. And after well-publicised trials alleging match-fixing by some famous Premier League players, at least one Asian gambling syndicate decided that technical sabotage would prove less risky than relying on footballers to throw matches.

Although he described himself as a professional gambler, in court Wai Yuen Liu was called a 'Mr Nobody', who in two years had lost £120,000 at the Golden Horseshoe casino in West London. It was reported that in April 1999 he was £30,000 in debt. When he was arrested police found about £3,000 cash in his pocket which officers believed was a down-payment to Firth.

The men in custody, the Charlton-Liverpool match went ahead. The FA's acting executive, David Davies, said,:

> Football may have been the intended target of an outside attack. That attack has been thwarted, for which we are very grateful. Football is determined to play its part in helping the police in every possible way. The football authorities are working together in doing so. The Premier League and

> the Football League will be contacting all clubs over the next twenty-four hours. The integrity of the game is crucial to us all. Jointly we are taking all steps to ensure that games go ahead normally this weekend.

Davies said that the FA had provided the police with a list of previous floodlight failures. 'But they assure us that it is far too early to link such incidents to this case or to allegations of connections between football and gambling.'

Six months later, a miniature model of a football ground, complete with four 4ft-high floodlights, was set up in front of the jury at Middlesex Guildhall Crown Court. Police electronics expert Mark Stokes produced a type of remote-control unit – the sort normally used to open electric garage doors – to control the lights on the model to demonstrate how floodlights could be sabotaged. Stokes told the court: 'We were able to actually turn off the lights at Charlton Football Club by just depressing a remote-control button.'

Prosecutor Mark Dennis told the court that electrical equipment including junction boxes, wire cutters and remote units, were found in a car being driven by Liu. Dennis said that the operation showed 'complete disregard to the damage that could be caused to the integrity of the professional game in this country'.

Ong and Lim, who had both pleaded guilty, were each sentenced to four years' imprisonment. It took a jury six hours to find Wai Yuen Liu guilty by a majority of 10-2. He was sent to prison for thirty months. Roger Firth, who had become a key prosecution witness during Liu's trial, received eighteen months' imprisonment.

The judge, Fabyan Peter Leaf Evans, told Lim and Ong: 'You were partners in a highly professional, technical, criminal operation for which no doubt you were both going to be paid a substantial financial reward, regardless of whether that device was used or not.' He told Firth: 'You couldn't resist the temptation of the £20,000 that was offered. You betrayed the trust of the club who had employed you for four years, you tried to involve another employee.'

Liu's role, said the judge, remained a 'slight mystery' after he drove the two Malaysians to the ground on 10 February. But the discovery of nearly £3,000 in cash on him was consistent with the view that he had the money to partly pay off Firth. Searches of his home had also uncovered faxes with reference to gambling, and bank details that showed large amounts of money passing through his account.

During Liu's trial it was revealed that he had links with a leading Triad figure. It was reported that Lieu lived with his wife and two young children in a Kensington house belonging to Yuk Oi Law, wife of Yan Ming Suen who had been arrested in Hong Kong over an illegal World Cup betting operation.

Wai Yuen Liu was indeed a particularly interesting figure whose business interests went far beyond betting on fixed football matches. After his trial at Middlesex Guildhall, newspapers revealed his previous record. They reported that in 1990, at Southwark Crown Court, he had been sentenced to five years' imprisonment for his involvement in a major criminal conspiracy after police found stolen and cloned credit cards and £50,000 in cash when they broke up what the press described as a 'gang of international forgers'. The gang was uncovered when a woman police officer spotted Lui and Yui Kar Au, described in court as a Hong Kong businessman, counting a huge amount of cash – £20,000 – on a train. When the pair alighted at London Bridge station she and her colleague, followed and arrested them. Later that day three more members of the gang were arrested. All were jailed.

Liu was released from prison in 1991. In December 1992, in a trial at the Old Bailey, he was one of five Chinese men acquitted of a charge of conspiring to cause grievous bodily harm to another Hong Kong businessman, Ying Kit Lam. Lam had been shot four times at close range in London's Chinatown during an alleged Triad power struggle.

Seven years later, Liu found himself in court yet again. This time charged with the football floodlights affair. After they had completed their jail terms the Malaysians were to be deported. Liu held a British passport. Outside the court, Detective Superintendent Andy Sellers of the Metropolitan Police's organised crime group, told reporters: 'I hope that today's verdict and the earlier pleas will serve as a very clear message to others that attacks on the national game of football will not be tolerated.'

When the 1997 abandoned matches were replayed, the outcomes were as everyone expected: West Ham beat Crystal Palace 4-1, and Wimbledon lost 1-0 to Arsenal. At the end of the season, Arsenal were crowned champions of the Premier League, and Crystal Palace were relegated. Free from the dangers of a floodlight failure, on

13 February 1999 Charlton, briefly back in the top-flight after an eight-year absence, beat Liverpool 1-0 at The Valley. Liverpool's Jamie Carragher was sent off in the sixty-eighth minute and, two minutes later, Charlton's Keith Jones beat the Reds' goalkeeper David James. At the end of the season, however, Charlton were still relegated.

Meanwhile, in a joint statement issued by the FA, the Premier League and the Football League, the game's authorities indulged in a bit of wishful thinking: 'The game was unknowingly the intended victim in this case. Football was being used as a vehicle for fraud in other areas of the world. With the outcome of today's trial, a clear message has been sent to anyone intending to use football for criminal activity.' It was a message that did not get through to everyone.

Chapter 11

A Decent Conspiracy Theory

> The referee was a disgrace. It was like something out of a comedy film. We are angry and disappointed. It's not fair that a country like Italy can be humiliated like this.
>
> Senator Raffaele Ranucci

Byron Moreno was just another referee. An international one, admittedly, but still just one of dozens whose names did not strike a particular chord. Until 18 June 2002. On that day Moreno took charge of the South Korea-Italy round-of-16 World Cup finals match in the city of Daejeon. And what a mess he made of it. In front of more than 38,000 spectators, millions of television viewers and the world's football media, too. Now everyone interested in the game would be familiar with the name of Byron Moreno from Ecuador.

The 2002 finals were co-hosted by South Korea and Japan, and the atmosphere in the Daejeon Stadium that evening was overwhelming. Thousands of home fans banged drums. Tens of thousands roared. The noise was ear-splitting. South Korea were a fast, skilful team managed by former Netherlands manager Guss Hiddink, who had been hired to give the co-hosts a boost for the World Cup. And he succeeded. When the Koreans beat Poland 2-0 it was their first ever victory in the first stage of a World Cup finals. A 1-1 draw with the United States and a 1-0 win against strongly fancied Portugal saw them top their group and progress into the second round where Italy stood in their way.

This was a great Italian side; from their goalkeeper Gigi Buffon, who had cost Juventus a world record transfer fee of more than £47 million, right through the team skippered by Paolo Maldini, one of the greatest defender in the game. Maldini had Fabio Cannavaro and Alessandro Nesta alongside him. A truly legendary defence. The midfield included Damiano Tommasi, who would one day become the mayor of Verona,

Italy's goalkeeper Carlo Ceresoli looks for help for a stricken England player during the 'Battle of Highbury' in November 1934. (Alamy)

Bodies lie on the pitch at Burnden Park, Bolton, after the sixth-round FA Cup-tie between Bolton Wanderers and Stoke City in March 1946 ended in the deaths of thirty-three spectators. (Alamy)

Above: Italy's Giorgio Ferrini is sent off by English referee Ken Aston during the 'Battle of Santiago' in 1962. (Alamy)

Left: Jimmy Gauld, the 'Judas who betrayed others' in the 1960s bribery and betting scandal that rocked football. (Alamy)

Armed police mix with players during the Racing Club–Celtic 'Battle of Montevideo' in November 1967. (Alamy)

Offenbach Kickers' president Horst-Gregorio Canellas (centre) watches as sound engineer Werner Hix plays incriminating tape recordings at Canellas's birthday party in June 1971. (Alamy)

Above: Juventus goalkeeper Din Zoff denies Derby County at the Baseball Ground as they try to get back into the 1973 European Cup semi-final. In the first leg, in Turin, Derby had been the victims of some skulduggery. (Author's Collection)

Left: Brian Clough, already angry at the hands of 'cheating bastards' when he was manager of Derby County, was cheated again when his Nottingham Forest side met Anderlecht in April 1984. (Author's Collection)

Algerian supporters wave money at photographers as their team goes out of the 1982 World Cup at the 'Disgrace of Gijon'. (Alamy)

Police and spectators on the pitch during the Heysel Disaster in May 1985. (Alamy)

Bernard Tapie (right), president of Olympique Marseilles, and AC Milan's president Silvio Berlusconi are friendly enough here. But relations would sour after the 1993 bribery scandal. (Alamy)

Bruce Grobbelaar and his wife Debbie leave Winchester Crown Court in January 1997. The former Liverpool goalkeeper was accused of attempting to fix football matches. (Alamy)

Kurt Röthlisberger attempts to calm players. In 1997, UEFA imposed a lifetime ban on Röthlisberger for attempted bribery. (Alamy)

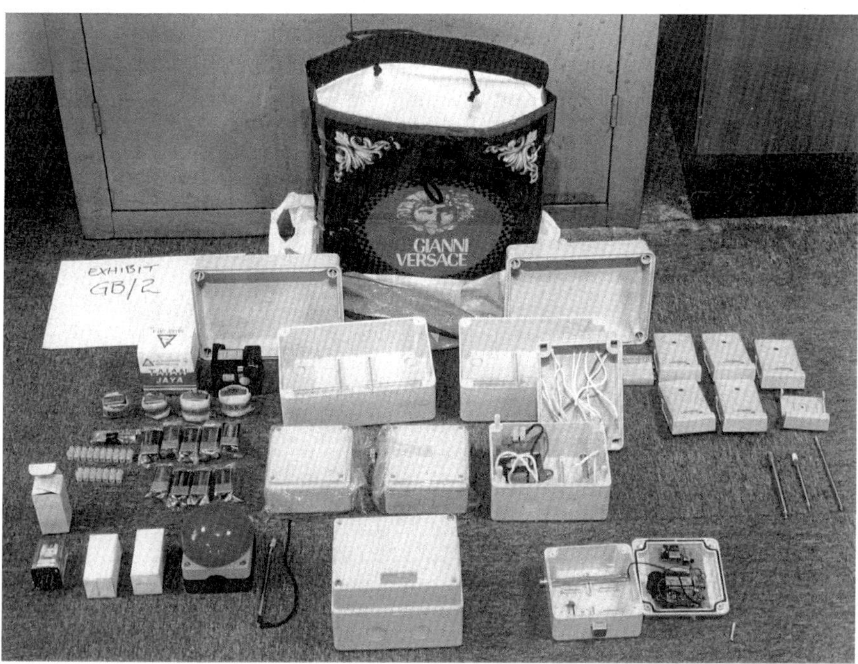

Metropolitan Police photograph of electrical equipment found in the hotel room of Chee Kew Ong and Eng Fwa Lim during the investigation into the sabotaging of the floodlights at Charlton Athletic's ground in 1999. (Alamy)

Above left: Referee Byron Moreno is confronted by Italy's Angelo Di Livio during the controversial 2002 World Cup match between Italy and South Korea in Daejeon. (Alamy)

Above right: Disgraced referee Robert Hoyzer on his way to the sports court at German Football Federation headquarters in 2005. (Alamy)

Luciano Moggi (left), the man at the centre of *Calciopoli* – 'Footballgate' – and AC Milan's CEO Adriano Galliani share a joke at the Italian Football Federation's general assembly in 2005. (Alamy)

and the versatile Gianluca Zambrotta. Up front Christian 'Bobo' Vieri, free-kick specialist Alessandro Del Piero, Francesco Totti and Pippo Inzaghi, or 'Superpippo' as AC Milan supporters liked to call him, supplied plenty of goals.

All those stars … Byron Moreno was undoubtedly the least well-known man on the pitch, but all that was about to change.

After four minutes Moreno awarded South Korea a penalty after Seol Ki-Hyun was adjudged to have been the victim of shirt-pulling by Christian Panucci. Ahn Jung-Hyun, who was on loan to Perugia in Serie A, stepped up to take the spot-kick and hung his head in his hands as Buffon dived low to tip his shot past the goalpost.

In the eighteenth minute Vieri gave Italy the lead with a powerful header from a corner and it seemed that the Italians would go into the quarter-finals. Two minutes from the end of normal time, however, Seol Ki-Hyun equalised to take the game into extra time.

In the 103rd minute Francesco Totti was sent off for 'diving', his second yellow card adding up to a red. Totti did go down rather easily but there was room for doubt. Moreno was some 40m (44yds) away. Totti was not only dismissed, he was denied the penalty he thought he should have had. VAR would have settled it. Maybe …

In the twentieth minute of extra time Tommasi looked to have scored a golden goal winner for the ten-man Italy, but his effort was ruled offside. Most observers thought that the goal should have stood and even Moreno later agreed, pinning the blame on linesman Jorge Ratallino.

Six minutes later, Ahn Jung-Hyun, the man who missed a fourth-minute penalty, outjumped Maldini to head past Buffon, and South Korea had their golden goal, although there was still time for Vieri to miss from six yards.

Then the accusations began. Bruno Pizzul, Italy's best-known commentator, summed it the general feeling: 'Frankly, that was complete robbery.' Italy's minister for public offices, Franco Frattini, went even further: 'The referee was a disgrace, absolutely scandalous. I've never seen a game like it. It seemed as if they just sat around a table and decided to throw us out.'

Raffaele Ranucci, head of the Italian football delegation to the World Cup, told Italy's RAI state television broadcaster (which threatened to sue FIFA for lost revenue after some of Moreno's decision were 'so blatant they could only be described as the product of serious fraud') that a conspiracy had taken place. 'Korea is a powerful country. It's clear that they would have done something. I've never in my life seen refereeing that bad.'

Italy's manager, Giovanni Trapattoni, was adamant as to what had just happened: 'We are going out in a bad way. Even the FIFA delegates that I know were incredulous. I don't speak of any conspiracy, but certainly of negative situations. These linesmen are incapable.'

The Italian players weighed in. Skipper Maldini:

> Mr Moreno whistled against us from the first minute to the last. It was a scandal. They wanted Italy out of the World Cup. You all saw what Moreno did. Before the beginning of the match Damiano Tommasi, a very polite guy, tried to greet him as he always does before every match. He offered his hand but Moreno turned around and refused to shake it.

Reserve goalkeeper Francesco Toldo: 'There has been a plot to put Italy out of the World Cup. The referee was ridiculous. The Ecuadorian referee's attitude was purposefully provocative.'

Guss Hiddink was obviously less likely to blame the referee or the linesmen: 'I'm very, very happy. Italy are one of the superpowers of world football. The Korean players keep on fighting and tactically they have learned a lot in just a few weeks. What they have done is unique.'

In the wake of the blistering criticism he was drawing from Italian media, Moreno hit back. He told the Chilean newspaper, *La Tercera*:

> Italians are talking about kickbacks or bribes because they use this form of corruption a lot. It reflects what they did or what they can do. The accusations are very strong and now they have to prove them. I heard what the Perugia president [Luciano Gaucci] said about the Korean scorer, Ahn. Well that gives you an idea of the Italians' moral weight. Italians are immature.

Moreno was referring to Gaucci cancelling Ahn's contract with the words: 'I have no intention of paying a salary to someone who has ruined Italian football.' Gaucci later took back what he had said and approved an option to sign Ahn on a permanent basis. This time it was the player's turn have his say: 'I will no longer discuss my transfer to Perugia who attacked my character instead of congratulating me for a goal in the World Cup.'

Moreno had not finished: 'I feel that I did a great job in the game. Italy are just looking for excuses to justify their elimination. They are hurt because they thought they were favourites to win this World Cup. But my conscience is clear.'

It was now open season on South Korea's success. When they beat Spain 5-3 on penalties to become the first Asian country to reach a World Cup semi-finals, there was talk of FIFA involvement. In the Dublin-based *Sunday Tribune*, Paul Howard wrote:

> It gets fishier and fishier ... Spain finally got their comeuppance for beating Ireland last weekend when they lost on penalties to Guss Hiddink's side, but only after having two perfectly good goals disallowed in a scoreless draw ... Teams from South America, Europe, Asia and Africa in the semi-finals ... Suspicious minds would have said it was the semi-final line-up FIFA might well have rigged. As it was there was enough of a dispute over South Korea's shock victory to add flesh to the bones of a decent conspiracy theory.

South Korea's penalty competition victory had come after Spain's Fernando Morientes had what looked like a legitimate golden goal in the second minute of extra time disallowed by Egyptian referee Gamal Al-Ghandour when a linesman signalled the ball out of play before Joaquin crossed it. Earlier in the game, Ruben Baraja had a second-half goal disallowed when Morientes was ruled offside. So, South Korea went through to the semi-finals where the 'plot' came to an end. They lost 1-0 to West Germany in Seoul, and the Germans lost 2-0 to Brazil in the Final in Yokohama.

And what of Mr Moreno? Three months after the World Cup finals had ended he was suspended for twenty matches by the Ecuadorian Football Federation after he made some remarkable timekeeping errors while refereeing a league match between LDU Quito and Barcelona SC. Moreno played thirteen minutes of stoppage time during which LDU turned a 3-2 deficit into a 4-3 victory. The fourth official had signalled only six minutes but Moreno kept playing until the Quito club finally went ahead. At the time, Moreno was running for election to the Quito city council. After returning from his suspension, he was suspended again after controversially sending off three players in one match. Shortly afterwards, FIFA released a statement: 'As a result of a number of controversies regarding referee Byron Moreno in Japan, Italy and South America over the past few months, FIFA has decided to launch an investigation into the affair.' Moreno announced that he had retired from refereeing.

That was not the last we had heard of him, though. On 21 September 2021, he was arrested at JFK airport in New York City while attempting to smuggle 6kg (more than 13lbs) of heroin which was hidden in his underwear. He was sentenced to two-and-a-half years' imprisonment, of which he served twenty-six months before returning to Ecuador where, ironically, he worked on a television programme analysing refereeing errors.

He told *La Gazzetta dello Sport*: 'After all this time, I still receive insults on social media from Italian fans, but my conscience is clear.' About the stoppage time incident he said: 'There were stoppages, a referee has to take those into account when giving injury time.' And of his arrest for smuggling drugs: 'That was an ugly day in my career. Everyone knows why I did it, I was threatened and forced to carry the heroin. My wife's life was in danger.'

When it came to South Korea versus Italy, even then he had no regrets:

> The referee, especially at that time before VAR, has a split-second to choose and act. I have no concerns, because I know none of my refereeing decisions influenced the result of that game … Italy made mistakes that day. Giovanni Trapattoni shouldn't have introduced Gennaro Gattuso [a defensive midfielder from AC Milan] rather than a striker. That's when Italy lost the game.

So now we know.

Chapter 12

A Hornets' Nest

> The gambling Mafia spied on me on the internet and caught my weakest point ... I'm ashamed about the whole thing.
>
> Robert Hoyzer

On 21 August 2004, supporters of SC Paderborn 07, a club in the third tier of German football, looked forward to the visit of top-tier Hamburg to the north German city. The match was in the first round of the DFB-Pokal, the German FA Cup. Hamburg had lost both their opening Bundesliga matches, and Paderborn's fans discussed – more in hope than expectation – whether a cup shock might be possible.

Half an hour into the game those hopes appeared to have been dashed as Hamburg led 2-0 with goals from German international midfielder Christian Rahm and Belgian international striker Emile Mpenza. But then fortunes began to turn.

Ten minutes before half-time, referee Robert Hoyzer, a distinctive fair-haired figure who stood 6ft 5in tall, awarded the home team a controversial penalty. Hamburg's players protested and in the ensuing argument Mpenza was sent off. Guido Spork scored from the spot and before half-time Rene Mueller equalised. On the hour, Daniel Cartus put the home side ahead, and although ten-man Hamburg threw everything at getting back into the game, eight minutes from the end Spork put the result beyond them after Hoyzer awarded Paderborn another dubious penalty. Final score 4-2 to the home team. While most of the 7,027 spectators in the Hermann-Löns-Stadion – Paderborn's then home was perhaps the only football ground to be named after a poet – went home happily discussing what had just happened, Hamburg were so embarrassed that the defeat led to the sacking of their coach, Klaus Toppmoller.

It would be fifteen years before the clubs met again competitively – and by then the 2004 match would be remembered for much more than a simple cup upset. It had unleashed the biggest scandal in German football since the 1970s when more than fifty players were found to have manipulated the results of Bundesliga matches. Even worse, the latest scandal had come in the run-up to Germany hosting the 2006 World Cup finals.

Even before the Paderborn-Hamburg match, Hoyzer's performances had begun to arouse concerns. Four referees – Lutz Michael Fröhlich, Olaf Blumenstein, Manuel Gräfe, and Felix Zwayer – went to the DFB with their suspicions. An investigation got under way – the DFB now took the precaution of not naming referees for some matches until the day before the game – and it was discovered that large sums of money had been wagered on several matches which Hoyzer had refereed. The 25-year-old had yet to officiate in the top division of the Bundesliga, but he was regarded as one of Germany's best young referees.

On 24 January 2005, Hoyzer, still denying the accusations levelled against him, stepped down as a referee. Three days later, however, he admitted the match-fixing charges and promised to fully cooperate with the ongoing investigation. Through his lawyer, Hoyzer said: 'The accusations made against me in public are true. I regret my behaviour profoundly and I excuse myself to the German soccer federation, my referee colleagues and all soccer fans.'

In addition to the Paderborn-Hamburg DFB Pokal tie, the DFB announced that second and third-tier league games were also being scrutinised. On 3 February, police raided the homes of three senior referees. At least twenty-five people, including fourteen players, were now believed to be involved in match-fixing. The investigations were leading to the very top of the game in Germany, and state prosecutors said that they were considering charges of 'illicit and organised deception' against the suspects.

Hoyzer's name now generated opprobrium across Germany. Journalist Paul Newman, writing in the *Irish Independent*, described Hoyzer as 'an unlikely figure of national hate'. He was, said Newman, 'sociable, good-humoured, tall and handsome with blond highlights in his hair and a permanent tan'.

The beans were well and truly being spilled now. Hoyzer had been a regular visitor to the Café King, a popular nightspot a few minutes' walk from Berlin's famed Kurfürstendamm. Its slogan was 'we bet you'll come back again'. There he would meet former semi-professional lower league footballer Ante Sapina, who was born in Germany of Croatian parents and who now ran a sports betting agency, and Ante's brothers, Filip and Milan. Over the next few years the Sapina name would feature large in the story of European match-fixing.

On 8 February 2005, on the German television station ZDF – in his first public appearance since the affair erupted – Hoyzer warned of the revelations yet to come: 'The DFB weren't aware of the scope of it all. They thought it would be limited to just one referee … it was like hitting a hornets' nest. I've got a lot of information.'

He told the *Johannes B. Kerner Show*:

> I was as pleased as punch. The great amounts of money blinded me. As a ref I was earning about €3,000 [£2,040] a month. Suddenly it was tens of thousands. It's humiliating to be in front of everyone who is involved in soccer … I'm afraid of going to jail. I know the Croatians are dangerous.

ZDF announced that as a safety precaution the studio audience had been screened. Hoyzer said that of the €67,000 (£45,560) he had received, he had returned €13,900 (£8,840) and lent €12,000 (£8,160). 'I don't have any more,' he said. 'All my accounts are frozen.'

Hoyzer's claim that the fixing of football matches was widespread was backed up not just referees but also by players. Former Energie Cottbus goalkeeper Georg Koch, who was now playing for MSV Duisberg, claimed to have turned down €20,000 (£13,600) to throw a 2 Bundesliga match against Jahn Regensburg the previous season.

It was now claimed that although Hoyzer's first attempt, a regional league fixture in May between Paderborn and Chemnitz, might have ended in failure, on the following two weekends he successfully engineered the results of two games in the same competition. Then came the Paderborn-Hamburg game, fixed, said Newman, 'in retrospect, foolhardy fashion'.

Felix Zwayer, a referee's assistant who ran the line in a number of Hoyzer's matches, was the first to notice his erratic decisions. When Hoyzer twice invited Zwayer to help fix matches, Zwayer's suspicions were confirmed and he alerted a colleague. When two other officials began to voice their suspicions, the four men collectively informed the DFB. Oddly, Zwayer would later be banned for six months for his involvement, including accepting a €300 (£204) bribe from Hoyzer before a game between Wuppertal and Werder Bremen. There was no evidence that Zwayer had intentionally made any incorrect decisions during the game, but the DFB ruled that he had behaved in a 'grossly unsporting" manner' in accepting the money and not acting sooner to report Hoyzer.

Elements of the 2005 scandal were still rumbling on sixteen years later. In December 2021, Borussia Dortmund's England international midfielder Jude Bellingham was fined €40,000 (£35,000) by the DFB for remarks he made after Zwayer had awarded two penalties against Borussia when they lost a Bundesliga match against Bayern Munich. Bellingham told ViaPlay, a leading streamer of sport: 'You give a referee, that has match-fixed before, the biggest game in Germany, what do you expect?' The 18-year-old Bellingham had some support. Manuel Gräfe, one of the four referees including Zwayer that had asked the DFB to look into Hoyzer, told *Zeit Magazin*: 'If you accept money once and then cover up Hoyzer's manipulation for six months, you shouldn't be refereeing professional football.' Zwayer's reputation was hardly damaged, however. After taking a break from refereeing, he was in charge of the 2024 European Championship semi-final between England and the Netherlands, a game in which Bellingham played.

Back in February 2005, the scandal began to ripple beyond Germany when Hoyzer confessed to fixing a pre-season friendly in July 2004 between Middlesbrough and Hansa Rostock. Although one report said that the plan to fix the Boro game was never carried out, Hoyzer admitted to the Berlin prosecutors that he had received €1,000 (£690) to fix the match in Rostock's favour. Rostock, who would be relegated from the Bundesliga that season, beat Boro, who would finish seventh in the Premier League, 3-1.

Hoyzer, who had altogether received payments of more than €67,000 (£45,560) as well as an expensive new plasma-screen television set – he also claimed that referees being entertained with visits to brothels before matches was 'standard practice' – was now singing like the proverbial canary. He told DFB investigators that the betting ring with which he had been involved operated far beyond a pre-season friendly match. It also fixed games in Austria and Greece and, indeed, 'could affect the whole of Europe'.

UEFA was already looking into a December 2004 UEFA Cup match between the oldest club in Greek football, Panionios, and Georgia's Dinamo Tbilisi. After being 1-0 down at half-time, Panionios won 5-2. Warren Lush, a spokesman for bookmakers Ladbrokes, said:

> We stopped betting on the game six hours before kick-off. We saw the big gamble coming. There was a lot of talk about a big gamble in internet chatrooms and on websites. There were a lot of sizeable bets on half-time/full-time outcomes, which you don't normally get. We have no evidence that the game was fixed but there was enough evidence of a big gamble for us to act.

Greek broadcaster SKAI TV reported that individuals in Georgia knew the final score two days before the match took place.

Although the investigation into that game was launched before Hoyzer came clean, a UEFA spokesman said: 'It might now have some link to the German refereeing investigation.'

In April 2005, the DFB banned Hoyzer for life for his central role in Germany's biggest match-fixing scandal for thirty years. A plan to fine him €50,000 (£34,000) was dropped but he was warned that he could still face a civil claim for damages over the DFB's agreement to pay a compensation package of €2 million (£1.36 million) to Hamburg for their rigged early exit from the DFB-Pokal (in October 2005, Hamburg also staged a Germany v China friendly international to help towards the loss of revenue they had suffered as a result of their defeat by Paderborn). In 2008 it was announced that, in an out-of-court settlement, Hoyzer had agree to pay the DFB €126,000 (£85,860) in damages at a rate of €700 (£476) per month for fifteen years, with the money going to charitable causes.

The DFB would also ban referee Dominik Marks for life after Hoyzer gave him up, alleging that Marks had been involved in fixing three matches late in 2004. Referee Torsten Koop received a three-month ban for not promptly reporting an approach from Hoyzer, who he said he thought was simply boasting, hence the delay. And, of course, as we have already seen, Felix Zwayer was banned for six months, although that was kept secret for several years.

In the autumn of 2005 came the criminal trial of the match-fixers. The Berlin State Court found Hoyzer – who said that he found the idea that so much money could be won from gambling as 'utopian' – guilty of fraud and sentenced him to twenty-nine months' imprisonment. Dominik Marks, 30, was given a suspended sentence of eighteen months. Ante Sapina – who it was alleged had made €750,000

(£510,000) on the Paderborn result alone – received thirty-five months in jail and his brothers, 38-year-old Filip and 40-year-old Milan, had suspended sentences of twelve and sixteen months respectively. Former Manchester City midfielder Steffen Karl, the first player to be arrested in connection with the match-fixing scandal, was tried separately over the manipulation of the May 2004 match between his club, Chemnitz, and Paderborn. Karl was given a nine-month suspended prison sentence and banned for eight months by the DFB.

There were other casualties caught up in the unsavoury business. Hoyzer told the court that the Paderborn captain, Dutch midfielder Thijs Waterink, had helped him during the Hamburg game. 'He said that after telling him, "Come on, 'Wink'. Do something,"' Waterink had collapsed in the penalty area so that Hoyzer could point to the spot. In April, Waterink had received a four-month ban from the DFB for accepting money before the match, and Paderborn sacked him.

A trio of players from Bundesliga club Hertha BSC, who were known to associate with the Sapina brothers, were questioned over allegations concerning their surprise 3-2 cup defeat by third-tier Eintracht Braunschweig but there was no proof that they had anything to do with manipulating the result of that or any other match.

There were many strands running through the whole affair, not least the DFB's apparent reluctance to investigate allegations because of subsequent bad publicity around the staging of a World Cup finals in a country where manipulating the results of football matches was seemingly commonplace. Even the chairman of an injured party, Hamburg SV's chairman Bernd Hoffmann, felt that 'we don't have to follow every pig that Hoyzer drives through the village,' although he was apparently referring to doubts raised over the validity of some of Hoyzer's claims which the disgraced referee had suddenly remembered after finding himself in custody.

In light of his confession, prosecutors had sought only a suspended sentence for Hoyzer but the presiding judge, Gerti Kramer, said that his was a 'serious crime', especially as he had recruited other referees. Federal Prosecutor Hartmut Schneider asked for the sentences against Hoyzer and the others involved to be overturned. Schneider said that the Berlin court did not properly examine previous rulings in similar cases and that it had made a 'remarkably superficial' decision because of public pressure to wrap up the case well before the World Cup finals.

In March 2006, still free pending an appeal, the ever-optimistic Robert Hoyzer announced that he was hoping to find a new career as a place-kicker for Berlin Adler, an American football club and one of the most successful in the German Football League. 'I've been training for a week,' he said, 'and I hope to sign a contract within the next few weeks. I don't have a future in football and have considered how best to use my abilities.'

A career in 'grid-iron' was not to be, however. In December 2006, the Federal Court of Justice in Leipzig confirmed all the convictions and length of sentences. The DFB president, Theo Zwanziger, said: 'The threat of two years in prison will make one or two people think before trying to influence a football match.' He said that the Leipzig ruling made it clear that the manipulation of football matches 'was no mere trifle but a scam punishable by law'.

Three years later, another investigation centred on some 200 football matches in nine different European countries, and once again the name of Ante Sapina was among those involved. The matches included not only domestic league games but also three in the Champions League and twelve in the UEFA Europa League. UEFA spokesman Peter Limacher described it as 'the biggest betting scandal in Europe'. One of the investigators, Andreas Bachmann, said that initial estimates put the illegal gains at about €10 million (£6.8 million) but that figure was 'the tip of the iceberg'. Police in Germany, Britain, Austria and Switzerland staged simultaneous raids on some fifty properties in the four countries and fifteen arrests were made in Germany and two in Switzerland. 'We at UEFA are stunned by the magnitude of this,' said Limacher.

In 2011 Sapina confessed to manipulating more than twenty games, including the 2010 World Cup qualifier between Lichtenstein and Finland and the Champions League qualifier between Debrecini VSC of Hungary and Italy's Fiorentina by bribing players and match officials. He was sentenced to five-and-a-half years in prison. In 2012, Germany's Federal Court of Justice ordered a retrial following appeals. In an April 2014 retrial in Bochum, Ante Sapina had his sentence reduced by six months. After his first conviction six years earlier, Sapina had promised: 'Now I will start a new life. The scandal chapter is done.' But the temptation of quick money had been too great for the former economics student to ignore.

Chapter 13

Brazil, Bribery and Murder

> It is the biggest blow to Brazilians' passion for football, and a scandal with international repercussions.
>
> Brazil's Special Action Group to Combat Organised Crime

Carlos Tevez was not a happy man. On 7 September 2005, his Corinthians team had just lost 3-2 to São Paulo. There he sat at the post-match press conference – wearing a Manchester United shirt to show, should anyone still be unaware, that he wanted to leave Brazilian football – complaining about the two female officials, Ana Paula de Oliveira and Maria Elisa Barbosa, who had run the line. 'When football gets more serious,' he told journalists, women shouldn't be taking part. A derby like that cannot have two women as referees. It is not disrespectful to women, but such a match has to be led by men. It's a question of capabilities.'

The Argentinian forward also accused Brazilian referees of discrimination, and that very afternoon, a victim of persistent heavy tackles, he had got himself sent-off after swearing at the referee who he felt was not protecting him.

That referee, Edílson Pereira de Carvalho, was already something of a colourful figure. His pre-match ritual was to raise his two cards, one red, one yellow, both personalised with the inscription Deus é Fiel, (God is Faithful) before praying in the centre-circle. As a young man he had wanted to be a player but a trial with São José, a club in the second tier of the São Paulo state league, did not lead to anything. In 1991, at the age of 29, he became a referee, and in 2000 joined the international ranks of FIFA officials. That year Carvalho took charge of both legs of the Copa Libertadores semi-final tie between Palmeiras and Corinthians. It seemed that his career was on an upward path.

Just over two weeks after the match that had so annoyed Carlos Tevez, the name of referee who had sent him off was on the lips of everyone involved in Brazilian football. Edílson Pereira de Carvalho was at the centre of a match-fixing scandal, and that Corinthians-São Paulo game was one of eleven suspected of being manipulated for the benefit of an internet betting ring.

It was the weekly news magazine *Veja* that blew the whistle on what was to become known as Máfia do Apito (literally 'The Whistle Mafia') or sometimes the Escândalo do Apito ('The Whistle Scandal').

On 27 September 2005, the game's overall ruling body issued a statement from its Zurich headquarters:

> FIFA has suspended worldwide and until further notice … Edílson Pereira de Carvalho in the light of the Brazilian federal police's decision to open a criminal investigation … The Brazilian football association has informed FIFA that it has also opened an investigation into the case and that it will take all the necessary measures to resolve the matter.

Carvalho had been due to act as the fourth official in a World Cup qualifying match between Uruguay and Argentina the following month.

Veja said that the scandal involved Carvalho and another referee, Paulo Jose Danelon. Police had set up phone taps and one of them involved a Serie A match between Vasco and Figueirense on 7 August 2005, which Vasco won 2-1. According to police, Carvalho, who was to referee that game, was heard to say: 'I am going to award a foul in the middle of the field and if anyone protests, I will send them off.'

Along with Danelon and a businessman named as Nagib Fayad, who was alleged to be one of the organisers of the gambling ring, Carvalho was arrested. A second businessman, Wanderlei Pololi, was later taken into custody after being named in Danelon's statement.

After five days of questioning, Carvalho was released on 29 September. As he made his way to a waiting car he was surrounded by television cameras, journalists and photographers, and he was slapped by an angry fan, a supporter of Corinthians, a club that had lost two matches that season – 4-2 to Santos and 3-2 to São Paulo – which Carvalho had refereed.

Public prosecutors alleged that as soon as he knew which match he would be refereeing that weekend, Carvalho had telephoned Fayad and offered to influence the result. Altogether he had taken charge of eleven matches in the Brazilian championship that season. Sometimes, said the prosecutors, he would call Fayad from the referee's dressing room less than an hour before kick-off. He was not always able to make good on his promise, however. On one July Sunday afternoon an outstanding performance by Figueirense's versatile forward, the Brazil international Edmundo, who scored a hat-trick in a surprise 4-1 win away to Juventude, scuppered Carvalho's best efforts.

Brazil's sporting tribunal would decide whether all or only some of the eleven games refereed by Carvalho would be replayed. Paulo Jose Danelon, who was not held in custody, had already admitted to fixing three matches in the São Paulo state championship that season. His lawyer, Paulo Rogerio Bonini, said: 'My client confessed that he falsified the results of the three games for which he received 30,000 reais (£7,500).'

Three days after being freed, Carvalho also came clean publicly. In a television interview on 2 October, he said: 'I was corrupted, I allowed myself to get taken by this easy money … I did it because I wanted to … I was wrong … I know that I am never going to referee another game again. I'm finished.'

He told his interviewer that he had first been approached the previous September and had initially refused to become involved. In February, however, he changed his mind and helped America-Sao Jose to a 4-1 win over Palmeiras in the São Paulo state championship. Carvalho was reported to be in debt to the tune of 40,000 reais (£10,000), and received between 10,000 reais (£2,500) and 15,000 (£3,750) reais for each match he fixed.

On the day of Carvalho's television interview the president of the Superior Court of Sports Justice, Luiz Zveiter, announced that, although Carvalho had claimed that he had not fixed every one, the results of all eleven matches in which he officiated in that season's domestic championship would be annulled and the games would be replayed. It was such a mess: the programme of matches was two-thirds of the way through. Inter Porto Alegre were top of the table with fifty-one points from twenty-eight matches with fourteen left to play. Corinthians and Fluminense were both one point behind Inter, who had been refereed once by Carvalho – a 3-2 win over Coritiba – while Fluminense were involved in two matches where Carvalho had officiated. The decision to annul the matches was obviously not going to be popular with some clubs, and five – Figueirense, Santos, Cruzeiro, Ponte Preta and Internacional – unsuccessfully appealed the decision. Santos, Cruzeiro and Internacional wanted each match to be judged individually rather than this blanket decision. Fans, too, were angry; not always because their team was affected but sometimes because they had subscribed to television packages or pay-per-view that included games alleged to be manipulated.

In November 2005, a court injunction was sought that the results of the eleven matches should not be annulled, but the request was rejected. Then another lawyer requested the annulment of the replayed matches, in which case Internacional would be the champions; if not, then Corinthians would take the title. It was decided that no club should be named champions, but in December the Brazil Football Confederation (CBF) ignored that and awarded the title to Corinthians. A temporary restraining order was issued by a civil court obliging the CBF to abide by the original decision not to name any club as champions, but both FIFA and the CBF forbade clubs from petitioning any court other than one set up solely for sporting arbitration to settle disputes directly related to a football match. The petition to annul the replayed matches was withdrawn, and Corinthians were allowed to retain what was their fourth Serie A title.

The affair would not go away, though. In Brazil referees were appointed by a draw held the Friday before each fixture. It was hardly a balanced approach, discrepancies were bound to occur, and from the beginning of the 2005 season in April until 12 October, one lucky referee, Wagner Tardelli, had refereed twenty-four matches, seven ahead of any other official. Carvalho described Tardelli as a 'sidekick' of Armando Marques, head of Brazil's national refereeing commission and a man who, in the 1970s, had himself been involved in a few controversies and errors while he was refereeing.

In December 2008, on the final day of the season, Tardelli was replaced as the referee for the decisive Brazilian championship match between Goiás and São Paulo. On its website, the CBF said:

> On Saturday morning, the CBF received an alert that an attempt was being made to manipulate the result of the São Paulo v Goiás game. A new draw was made for the

> match in question, despite recognising the honesty and good character of referee Wagner Tardelli, who in twenty years of refereeing has always demonstrated the most correct behaviour and conduct. The president of the CBF has ordered the legal department … to take all appropriate actions to.. identify those responsible for this attempt to manipulate the game.

Goiás were officially at home but the match was being played in Brasilia as they began a two-match home ban following an incident in a previous game. Tardelli said: 'I'm ready and capable of refereeing the match. But, as a result of this incident … the CBF did the right thing in holding a new draw. I'm more interested than anyone else in seeing that the facts come to light.' São Paulo won 1-0 to take the title three points ahead of Grêmio who beat Atlético Mineiro to no avail. There was no suggestion of any wrongdoing and Tardelli continued his distinguished career.

Meanwhile, there was still the Carvalho business to conclude. In February 2011, a civil court ruled that the CBF, together with Carvalho and Fayad, would be fined a total of 160 million reais (about £70 million) based on a law that protected consumers' right, although it was not clear how the fine would be divided between them. They were found guilty of 'moral prejudices inflicted on supporters'. Together with Paulo Jose Danelon they were also found guilty of colluding together and ordered to pay a further 20 million reais (about £9 million).

Again, it was not clear how the fines would be divided between them but, speaking the following month, Carvalho, who was now working behind a bar in Jacareí, a city known as 'the Capital of Beer', seemed to be amused by the ruling.

He told the website *www-terra-com.br*,

> I was and remain super calm. I don't have that money to pay. It will be left up to the CBF and the São Paulo Federation. Let them sue each other. I will continue living my life and they will continue living their life … From what I've seen the process will take eight to twelve years. By then a lot will happen and Del Nero [Marco Polo Del Nero, then president of the São Paulo Football Federation] and Teizeira [Ricardo Teixeira, president of the CBF] will have already died.

In fact, the pair's downfall would come long before their ultimate demise. In November 2019, FIFA banned Teixeira for life after its ethics committee found him guilty of taking bribes linked to South American football competitions from 2006 to 2016, the year he resigned from FIFA's executive committee. He was also fined one million Swiss francs (£775,000). Teixeira's father-in-law, João Havelange, the Brazilian lawyer who was FIFA president from 1974 to 1988, was also involved, the pair allegedly pocketing more than 41 million Swiss francs (£21 million) in bribes in connection with the awards of World Cup marketing rights. And in September 2021, Del Nero, who had eventually followed in Teixeira's footsteps as CBF president, learned that his life ban from the sport had been reduced to twenty years, which meant that he would be 97 when it expired in 2038. The Court of Arbitration for Sport confirmed FIFA's case against Del Nero 'as to the findings on the merits', but ordered a reduced ban for taking bribes.

Between Teixeira's and Del Nero's reign (which lasted for only eight months, from April to December 2015), Jose Maria Marin served as CBF president. In May 2015, Marin was arrested in Zurich along with six other high-ranking FIFA officials accused of corruption and bribe taking. In December 2017, after a six-week trial, a US federal court, found him guilty of six of the seven counts against him of money laundering, wire fraud and conspiratorial racketeering. In August 2018, he was sentenced to four years' imprisonment (he had already served thirteen months), fined $1.2 million (£950,000) and ordered to forfeit $3.34 million (£2.6 million) In April 2019, he was banned by FIFA from all football-related activities and fined one million Swiss francs (£760,000). FIFA's investigation into Marin was linked with the awarding of contracts for the media and marketing rights to South American Football Confederation (CONMEBOL), Confederation of North, Central America and Caribbean Association Football (CONCACAF) and CBF competitions in 2012–15.

So, no less than three former CBF presidents were widely seen as part of a widespread corrupt culture. The affair had divided opinion among some of the most famous names in Brazilian football. In June 2015, Romário, a member of Brazil's 1994 World Cup winning team, who had recently been elected to the Brazil Senate with the most votes ever received by a candidate representing the state of Rio de Janeiro, said that Del Nero 'should call the press in and announce he is leaving the CBF'.

His views were supported by another former Brazil international, Leonardo, who called the CBF 'dirty'. And Ronaldo, who at 17 years of age had been the youngest member of the 1994 World Cup winning squad, also demanded that Del Nero resign immediately. Some of Ronaldo's former teammates saw that as simple opportunism from a man who was a member of the 2014 World Cup Organising Committee. Edmílson, a teammate of Ronaldo's when Brazil won the 2002 World Cup, told the São Paulo newspaper *Folha*. 'Ronaldo participated in the organising of the whole World Cup. And now he wants to get rid of Del Nero and Marin who were there with him?' Cafu, captain of the 2002 team, agreed. He told *Folha*: 'They are being accused and haven't been found guilty. So it's better to keep quiet and see what happens.'

In the meantime, it seemed that there was about the same chance as the proverbial snowball's in hell of Carvalho ever paying off his debts. In May 2023, *Veja*, the publication that had exposed the scandal eighteen years earlier, reported that the previous March, Luiz Gustavo Esteves, a judge from the 11th Civil Court of São Paulo, asked various bodies if Carvalho had any private pensions that could be seized. The response was negative. Previous searches of Carvalho's bank account, which had been frozen by a magistrate, revealed that there was not a single cent to be had. Lawyer Ricardo Di Giaimo said: 'Many years have passed and nothing has been received by the creditor to corroborate the popular jargon "you win but you don't take it".'

And so it went on. Betting on sport was not legalised in Brazil until 2018 when the country allowed online gambling. One of the most popular ways of laying a bet was to wager on red and yellow cards being shown and penalties being awarded.

In June 2023, Santos announced that they had terminated the contract of 27-year-old defender Eduardo Bauermann, who had been implicated in yet another match-fixing scandal that rocked Brazilian football after police in the state of Goias discovered a syndicate interfering with first and second tier matches. According to the Goias public prosecutor, at least fifteen matches had been fixed in 2022, including eight in the top tier.

Bauermann had agreed to get himself sent off in a game against Avaí FC on 5 November 2022, but he changed his mind and returned the money paid by a gambler who had bet on Bauermann's dismissal. Bauermann posted a video in which he said he wanted to 'ask forgiveness from the club, team-mates and the supporters'. He added: 'I am penalised the most, even while repenting and having done nothing of what I was proposed to do to harm my team.' Having ultimately turned down the bribe, he was given only a twelve-match ban by the Superior Court of Sports Justice.

This latest betting scandal had ramifications beyond Brazil. The Colorado Rapids Brazilian midfielder, 22-year-old Max Alves, who had joined the Major League Soccer (MLS) club from Flamengo before the start of the 2022 season, was not named but in May 2023 Rapids placed him on 'administrative leave' after it was alleged that he had been paid 60,000 reais (just under £10,000) for contriving to receive a yellow card in a MLS game against LA Galaxy in September 2022.

FIFA, meanwhile, endorsed lifetime bans on three Brazilian players – Ygor Catatau, Gabriel Tota, and Matheus Gomes – for their involvement in match-fixing. Eight other players were given suspensions of between one and two years.

CBF president Ednaldo Rodrigues said in a statement: 'I've been working together with FIFA, as well as with Brazilian clubs and federations, with the aim of combating all types of crime, fraud or illicit action within football. Those who commit crimes should not be part of Brazilian and world football.'

Not all the scandals in Brazilian football have been about fixing matches, however. In October 2021, São Paulo RS player William Ribeiro was charged with attempted murder after he attacked referee Rodrigo Crivellaro fourteen minutes into the second half of a Monday evening Campeonato Gaúcho Série A2 league game against Guarani-VA at the Edmundo Felix Stadium in Venâncio Aires.

Video footage showed Ribeiro attack Crivellaro after the referee did not award his team a free-kick. Crivellaro fell to the ground and Ribeiro is shown kicking the official on the head. Crivellaro lay motionless and was taken to hospital. Ribeiro was removed to the Venâncio Aires State Penitentiary.

The president of Ribeiro's club, Delvid Goulart, issued a statement:

> Unfortunate, regrettable and, above all, revolting. On the exact day when all the red and green family gather together to celebrate the 113th anniversary of São Paulo RS, our club faced one of the saddest episodes of its history, a fateful scene that shocked all people who love not only Gaúcho

> football but all those who just love sport on general. We send all the apologies in the world to the injured referee and his family as well as apologising to the public in general for the lamentable scene seen today. The contract of the offending player is terminated.

Astonishingly, the match was resumed the following day – and for the record, Guarani won 1-0. A few days later, Rodrigo Crivellaro was discharged from hospital. The 30-year-old William Ribeiro was released on police bail and subsequently banned for two years by the First Disciplinary Commission of the Rio Grande do Sul Court of Sports Justice, which meant that his playing career was effectively over. The Brazilian news outlet *UOL* reported that Ribeiro had previously attacked another referee and a supporter.

After his suspension was announced, he appeared contrite:

> There were several issues on the field. I made a mistake. What I did was not right. I'm very sorry. At the time I had a blackout and I acted like that. I can't explain what happened to me at the time. It just darkened my eyes. I'm even looking for psychological treatment.

Nine months after the Crivellaro incident it was reported that Ribeiro was playing in a seven-a-side game when he punched yet another referee.

For all the scandals that have bedevilled Brazilian football, however, there can be none more shocking than the events of 30 June 2013 in Pio XII in northern Brazil. The town is named after Pope Pius XII but the events of that Sunday afternoon were anything but papal.

A 20-year-old referee called Otávio Jordão da Silva was officiating in an amateur match when he was verbally abused by a 31-year-old player, Josenir dos Santos Abreu. Da Silva sent him off, but Abreu refused to leave the field. The ensuing argument saw the player throw a punch at the young official. During the fist fight that followed, da Silva drew a knife and stabbed Abreu. The player died on the way to hospital. As if that was not horrifying enough, what happened next beggars belief.

When news of Abreu's death reached those relatives and friends who had been watching the game, some of them ran on to the pitch and attacked da Silva. He was beaten to death, after which he was decapitated, his body quartered, and his head placed on a stake on the centre-spot. A 27-year-old man was arrested on suspicion of assault but it seems that so many were involved that no one was ever brought to trial.

In 2012, the legendary Pelé, an ambassador for the World Cup finals to be held in his home country two years hence, said: 'Brazil eats, sleeps and drinks football. It lives football. There's a huge sense of expectation and ambition to match.' What a pity that such passion for the game had so often been abused.

And what a shame it was that, in December 2023, supporters of Santos, the club that Pelé had graced for almost two decades, set fire to cars and buses as they rioted in response to Santos's first relegation from the Brazilian top-flight in 111 years.

Chapter 14

Calciopoli and Other Italian Jobs

> Our sales rocketed by about 50,000 copies a day since this happened. Even old women going to the market in the morning want to read about this. It is astonishing.
>
> *La Gazetta dello Sport* journalist Giancarlo Galavotti, speaking to BBC Sport.

In May 2006, Juventus headed towards their twenty-ninth Serie A title, and Italy's national team prepared for that year's World Cup finals in Germany. But Italian newspaper headlines were dominated by the most remarkable widespread corruption that football had ever seen.

It became known as Calciopoli – 'Footballgate' as in 'Watergate' – and at the centre of it all was a man of humble beginnings and fine tastes. Luciano Moggi, the former deputy railway stationmaster of a small Tuscan town, had risen to become one of the most powerful men in Italian football. Charm and an undoubted ability for spotting talent had enabled him to rise to the top of the Italian game, and he was now the general manager of the 'Old Lady', as Juventus was known.

This epic scandal was uncovered almost by accident. Investigators had been looking into several unrelated cases in Naples, in Turin and in Rome. They uncovered a multitude of alleged sins including a betting ring involving players and referees, doping, and also the affairs of a football agency, GEA World, that was owned by Moggi's son, Alessandro. The agency had some 200 players and coaches on its books and close links to Juventus. Magistrates ordered phone taps, including those on a number of mobile phones belonging to Luciano Moggi.

The daily *Gazzetta dello Sport* reported that 'the world of football is even more worried'. And, indeed, it should have been. Investigators discovered much more than they were looking for. Conversations between Serie A club presidents and officials of refereeing organisations, and between the clubs and referees themselves, pointed to something even bigger. Moggi's name cropped up more than most. And Juventus was more involved than any other club. It was an astonishing business, totally unexpected, and it would bring the football authorities, and the criminal justice system, crashing down on the top flight of Italian football. And all this in a World Cup year.

Moggi, a former chief executive with Roma, Lazio and Torino, had joined Juventus from Napoli in 1994. By then the Old Lady had won twenty-two Serie A titles, but only one of them had come in the previous nine seasons. Along with chairman Antonio Giraudo and former Juventus star Roberto Bettega as vice-president, Moggi led the club to renewed glory with six Serie A titles and one European Champions League trophy. Juventus's managers during that time make a short but impressive list: Marcello Lippi, Carlo Ancelotti and Fabio Capello, although Ancelotto's twenty-eight-month tenure at the Stadio Delle Alpi did not bring a major trophy – he did win the Intertoto Cup in his full first season – and in June 2001 he was sacked.

In May 2006, another Serie A title, the seventh under Moggi, was only a few days away for Juventus when *Gazzetta dello Sport* and *Corriere della Sera* began publishing transcripts of recorded phone taps that had been released by the police. One in particular, between Moggi and the vice-chairman of UEFA's referees committee, Pierluigi Pairetto, appeared to sum up an arrangement to appoint referees who would be likely to favour Juventus. When Pairetto rang Moggi to tell him that he had put in 'a great referee for the Amsterdam game' – the September 2004 Champions League group match against Ajax – Moggi replied: 'Well done!' The referee in question was the Swiss official Urs Meier, but although Juventus won the game 1-0 there was never any suggestion that Meier had favoured them and he was never investigated.

The entire nature of Pairetto's call suggested that he was pandering to Moggi. He began it with: 'Hey! Have you forgotten me? I always remember you.' And ended with: 'I only called to tell you that. See, I remember you.' Moggi replied: 'Oh, don't break my balls. You'll see that when I'm back you'll realise that I haven't forgotten you.' Quite what was the nature of Pairetto's reward, if any, was not clear. But Moggi was a powerful figure in Italian football and could influence careers. There was the story that he once had referee Gianluca Paperesta and his assistants locked in a dressing-room toilet at Reggina's Stadio

Oreste Granillo after he was less than pleased with the way that they had officiated a game. So Moggi was not man to have as an enemy.

Earlier in that 2004–05 Champions League campaign, after expressing dismay at the way a qualifying round game against the unfancied Swedish club Djurgaarden had been refereed –after Juventus had a goal disallowed the Swedes held on for a 2-2 draw – Moggi gave his choices for the referee and assistant referee appointments for a forthcoming friendly match against Messina. He named his favoured officials and Pairetto replied: 'Done already!' None of the men appointed was suspected of any offence. Pairetto then assured Moggi that Juventus would win the second leg against Djurgaarden, 4-1. And so they did. In the twenty-four hours before a game between Juventus and AC Milan, police found no less than thirteen phone calls between Moggi and the match referee.

On 5 May 2006, four Italian referees were suspended. Four days later, the president of the FIGC, Franco Carraro, resigned after it was reported that it had taken no action about the transcripts, despite being aware of them since February. Carraro was followed out of the door first by Innocenzo Mazzini, the vice-president, and then by Tullio Lanese, the president of the Italian referees' association, the Associazione Italiana Arbitri.

The scandal was reaching every corner of the game. Aldo Biscardi, host of Italy's most popular television football show, resigned after allegations that he had collaborated with Moggi to boost Juventus's image. Italian newspapers published excerpts of phone conversations between Moggi and Biscardi in which the presenter is allegedly pressured into favouring Juventus. Biscardi said that he had decided to leave because of 'all that is happening in the soccer world'.

The transcripts covered more than 100,000 conversations recorded over an eight-month period. And it was not just Juventus that was involved. Police had uncovered similar conversations between referees' officials and other club officials. AC Milan, Fiorentina and Lazio were also named. Investigating magistrates in Naples described it as 'a cupola of power marked by alliances between the managers of some big clubs, agents and referees'.

Massimo de Santis, an Italian referee due to officiate in the World Cup finals, withdrew from the competition. The 44-year-old's day job was working as a police constable. Assistant referees Alessandro Griselli and Marco Ivaldi had their accreditation withdrawn by the FIGC.

On 11 May, the entire Juventus board of directors resigned. Three days later, Juventus lifted another Serie A title. Moggi was not there to celebrate, however. He, too, had resigned, telling journalists: 'I miss my soul. It has been killed. From this day the world of football is no longer my world.'

When the news first broke, former Juventus striker Gianluca Vialli, who was now working as a television pundit, said: 'The fear I have when I read these things is that we are dealing with the tip of the iceberg and the worst is yet to come.'

On 23 May, a 76-year-old retired magistrate, the Naples-born Francesco Borelli, was asked by the FIGC to take on the investigation. A former chief prosecutor of Milan, Borelli was a formidable figure. In the 1990s his forensic investigation into local corruption had led to the collapse of the entire political system that had ruled Italy since the Second World War. Now he returned to judicial work as the head of an investigation into football corruption. Borelli worked quickly to pass on his findings to sporting public prosecutor Stefano Palazzi.

On 27 June 2006, two days before the sporting trial was due to begin in an improvised courtroom at Rome's Olympic Stadium, Juventus's new manager, their former player, 35-year-old Italian international Gianluca Pessotto, fell 15m (50ft) from a dormer window in the roof of the club's four-storey headquarters in Turin. Pessotto fell into an inner courtyard and suffered multiple fractures and internal haemorrhaging. Police said that he was clutching rosary beads and they were treating the incident as a possible suicide attempt. His wife, Reanna, later said that he had simply blacked out. Pessotto would recover well enough to resume his managerial duties.

On 29 June, Stefano Palazzi laid out his charges to an 81-year-old former judge of the Constitutional Court of Italy, Cesare Ruperto. The first day was taken up by procedural matters and after lawyers asked for more time to study documents, Ruperto adjourned proceedings with the warning: 'We must go straight to our objective, which is justice. We've received a request for postponement from five third parties involved – Bologna, Messina, Lecce, Treviso and Brescia.' He said that while the request for this postponement would be accepted, there would be no further delays. Luciano Moggi was not in court to hear any of this. He had not appeared. Adriano Galliani, the CEO of AC Milan, was no shrinking violet, however. He sat himself on the front row to hear the charges brought against his club.

Palazzi wanted AC Milan, Lazio and Fiorentina to be relegated to Serie B – and Juventus to be sent down two divisions to Serie C.

While all this was going on, Juventus players were helping Italy to win the World Cup. Juve's Alessandro Del Piero scored the winner of a pulsating semi-final against Germany in Dortmund. Four days later, Italy's captain, Fabio Cannavaro of Juventus, lifted the trophy when France were beaten on penalties after a 1-1 in Berlin's Olympic Stadium.

The World Cup had taken exactly one month to complete. The court case was over in only five days, two of them taken up by procedural wrangling. In all, twenty-six defendants – club and FIGC officials, referees and assistant referees – pleaded their case. The verdicts of five retired judges were delivered and now everyone awaited the sentences. Not everyone was out for blood. Italy's justice minister, Clemente Mastella, repeated calls for the clubs to be let off. 'Let us do what they did in Ancient Rome. Whoever has given us prestige and dignity should be treated differently,' he said.

It was going to be the same justice for everyone, however, no matter how much prestige and dignity they might have delivered. On the hot Friday evening of 14 July 2006, Cesare Ruperto read out those sentences. Juventus had escaped a drop into the third tier, but the great champions would still begin the 2006–07 season in Serie B. At news of the sentences, outside Juventus's offices in central Turin supporters of their local rivals, Torino, drove past sounding their car horns and shouting, 'Relegate them to Serie Z.' Torino had recently won promotion back to Serie A.

Lazio and Fiorentina were also to be relegated but AC Milan escaped with a fifteen-point deduction, which meant that they had not qualified for Europe. The judges also ruled that Juventus would start the Serie B season with a huge thirty-point deduction, but this was later reduced to nine on appeal. AC Milan's points deduction was also reduced so that they qualified for the Champions League after all. Lazio and Fiorentina were reprieved and were back in Serie A, albeit with a big points deduction and no European football for the following season. In August, in a second wave of Calciopoli investigations, another Serie A club, Reggina, also received a points deduction, as did Serie B club AC Arezzo. Reggina were also fined €100,000 (£68,000).

But the biggest blow for Juventus was that not only were they stripped of their 2004–05 Serie A title (which was left undesignated), they also lost the 2005–06 title. The 'Scudetto di cartone', the 'cardboard Scudetto' as it became known, was handed to Inter Milan. Juventus never contested losing it but they fought hard – and unsuccessfully – to take it away from Inter.

Despite losing manager Fabio Capello, who had resigned as the scandal unfolded, and being forced to transfer star players – Patrick Viera and Zlatan Ibrahimovic moved to Inter Milan; World Cup-winning captain Fabio Cannavaro went to Real Madrid along with Emerson; Gianluca Zambrotta and Lilian Thuram signed for Barcelona; Adrian Muto to Fiorentina – Juventus retained enough talent to overcome their minus-nine-points start to 2006–07, and returned to Serie A at the first attempt, as champions of the second tier.

AC Milan – managed by Carlo Ancelotti, the man who was judged to have failed at Juventus – not only recovered their Champions League place, they went on to win the trophy, beating Liverpool 2-1 in the Final in Athens.

Some twenty individuals were also punished by the sporting court. Luciano Moggi was suspended from football for five years and fined €50,000 (£34,000) with the recommendation that he be banned for life from any level of the FIGC (in June 2011, along with Juventus's Antonio Giraudo, and former FIGC vice-president Innocenzo Mazzini, both of whom had also initially received a five-year ban, Moggi senior would indeed be banned from football for life). Pierluigi Pairetto, that most accommodating of referees' officials, was banned for two-and-a-half years (later increased to three-and-a-half). Massimo de Santis, who should have refereed in the World Cup finals, was banned for four years. Former FIGC president Franco Carraro received a four-year suspension.

Following the sporting trial in Rome, criminal proceedings eventually began in Naples, signalling a long and complicated affair that dragged on for six years. In March 2015, the *Football Italia* website reported: 'The final verdict in the long-running Calciopoli trial has been confirmed with some charges dropped and others affected by the statute of limitations.'

After six hours of deliberation, the verdicts were announced by the Supreme Court of Cassation, Italy's highest appeal court. Luciano Moggi was cleared of two counts of sporting fraud, while a sentence of two years' imprisonment for criminal conspiracy was written-off because the statute of limitations had expired and the sentence could not now be enforced. So he had been cleared of some individual charges but not from being the 'promoter' of the conspiracy that culminated in Calciopoli.

Antonio Giraudo would also avoid a prison sentence (one year and eight months for fraud) thanks to the statute of limitations.

Two former referees, Paolo Bertini and Antonio Dattilo, were acquitted but an appeal by Massimo De Santis, who had already accepted a ten-month suspended prison sentence, was rejected. De Santis, who had missed officiating in the 2006 World Cup, was more than miffed at this latest setback: 'I wouldn't wish this kind of justice on anyone. It seems to me like I've been discriminated against. Now I'm waiting to read the motivations, I want to understand why I was the only referee involved.' The prosecution's appeal against the acquittals of referees Paolo Dondarini, Gianluca Rocchi and Tiziano Pieri as well as that of Tullio Lanese, the former president of the Associazione Italiana Arbitri, were declared inadmissible.

In 2009, Luciano Moggi had declared: 'What is Calciopoli? Calciopoli is just errors made by referees. The truth is that Calciopoli never existed.' Now he insisted that these rulings finally proved that Serie A was not fixed: 'This has been an unpleasant thing, and it's all ended up in nothing. In nine years it's been established that the league was regular, the selection [of the referees] was regular and that there were no communications.'

In September 2015, the Supreme Court of Cassation published a 150-page document explaining the reasons for its final ruling on the criminal charges relating to Calciopoli. It said that Luciano Moggi had 'unjustified and excessive power' within Italian football. He was guilty of 'guiding a significantly structured association widely diffused across the whole territory with every single person involved fully aware'. It described him as the 'initiator of an illicit system influencing matches in the 2004–05 season (and not only this one)'. It said that Moggi exerted 'an extraordinary amount of power also in the fields of journalism and television' which enabled him to get away with 'fraudulent activity in favour of the club he belonged to'.

So the criminal case was over. Civil actions still took place, however, and Juventus tried hard to have the 2005–06 Serie A title removed from Inter Milan. In 2022, that battle was finally lost when further appeals were deemed inadmissible. The 2015 ruling also put paid to the Old Lady's plan to sue the FIGC for material and moral losses estimated to be in the region of €443 million (£301 million). In 2016, a TAR (Tribunali Amministrativi Regionali – Regional Administrative Court) tribunal in Lazio rejected Juventus's appeal against the Italian Olympic Committee for its refusal to pay compensation. The TAR statement read:

> The entire issue has already been dealt with in a previous claim, presented also by Juventus, in 2006 and then abandoned by the club, who preferred instead to take it to arbitration, where they did not succeed ... The TAR cannot deliberate on something that arbitration has already deliberated on.

When, in May 2006, the Dublin-based *Evening Herald* headlined the breaking news of Calciopoli, 'Another Week, Yet Another Scandal In Italy', no one could have imagined for how long the story would run.

There had, of course, been scandals in Italian football before, plenty of them, not least the 1980 Totonero affair which saw an Italian greengrocer, Massimo Cruciani, and his restaurateur friend, Alvaro Trinca, have the audacity to complain that footballers they had bribed to fix matches had defrauded the pair by failing to deliver the required results. On 23 March 1980, police carried out a number of raids on football stadiums around Italy, and some players were arrested as they left the field.

After Cruciani and Trinca lifted the lid, twenty players were banned, some indefinitely, by the FIGC, including Paolo Rossi who would survive the scandal and go on to be a member of the Azzurri team that won the 1982 World Cup. AC Milan and Lazio were relegated to Serie B, with other clubs in Italy's top two divisions receiving points deductions.

The Totonero affair was named for the state-run competition, similar to Britain's football pools, that was then the only legal form of betting on football in Italy. To win it was necessary to predict the results of twelve matches, far too many to all be fixed. But, of course, with illegal bookmakers it was possible to bet on individual games.

Totonero reared its head again in 1986 when Turin police monitoring the phone calls of suspected drug traffickers, accidentally uncovered another match-fixing scandal that involved clubs in several tiers of Italian football, together with players, managers and coaches, and even club presidents. One of the most damning results of a phone tap was when an illegal bookmaker was heard to say that Tito Corsi and Italo Allodi, directors of Udinese and Napoli respectively, were 'in agreement for a draw'. The bookmaker suggested that Napoli's Diego Maradona could be a problem, though. The brilliant Maradona might invent 'a goal all of his own'.

'All we need to do now is invent something to get Maradona sent off,' he continued. 'Criscimanni is available. He is willing to provoke the Argentinian.' In the ensuing match, in November 1985, it took Maradona only nine minutes to invent a brilliant goal. Twenty minutes later, however, he was crudely felled by Udinese's Antonino Criscimanni. Maradona got to his feet, headbutted Criscimanni and was sent off. The game ended 1-1, the draw that Corsi and Allodi had agreed. After the investigation into that and many other instances was completed, Udinese were relegated from Serie A, eight other clubs were punished for similar offences, and dozens of individuals were suspended for various lengths of time.

Then there was Calciopoli – and only five years after that another scandal which saw Italian football yet again marred by allegations of match-fixing. In May 2011, police descended upon the Italian national team's training camp in Tuscany. The 6.40am raid led to the arrest of sixteen people – current and recently retired footballers, club executives and bookmakers – thought to be connected to a Bologna-based betting ring.

Seventeen matches in Serie B and lower league football were the focus of a six-month investigation – 'Operation Last Bet' – that had begun after a third-tier match between Paganese and Cremonese in November 2010, when it was alleged that Cremonese players had their half-time drinks spiked with a sleeping drug. After this latest investigation, fifteen clubs were penalised. Only one of them, Atalanta, was from Serie A, and they were docked six points from the 2011–12 season. Dozens of players received bans from football ranging from one to five years.

Regarding criminal proceedings, prosecutor Roberto Di Martino explained that in Italy 'it's considered a minor type of fraud – sports fraud – which is penalised with sentences of a maximum of two years'. Sentences up to two years were generally suspended anyway, and before any criminal prosecutions proceeded, many of those accused of match-fixing had already faced disciplinary hearings by sporting bodies.

In 2013, Di Martino said: 'Let's hope it's a starting point for cleaning up the beautiful game that is football.' Two years later, more than fifty people, one of them a police officer, were arrested throughout Italy as part of an investigation into dozens of alleged fixed third- and fourth-tier matches. Prosecutors in the southern town of Catanzaro were looking at a network of players, managers, coaches and club presidents involving more than thirty clubs. Police said that some of those charged had links to Mafia organisations. There seemed to be no end to the Italian jobs …

Chapter 15

Match Fixing in the K-League

> There is a danger that people feel that the storm has passed and most footballers involved in this match-fixing don't feel guilty, but unlucky.
>
> Journalist Seo Hyung-wook, talking to Associated Press.

In late June 2011, South Korean international striker Choi Sung-kuk became the latest player to confess to involvement in a growing match-fixing scandal that threatened to engulf Asia's oldest professional league. Tragically, it was also a scandal that would claim the lives of at least four people.

Bribery and corruption in South Korean football was relatively new. The K-League was not formed until 1983 and it took twenty-five years before, in 2008, allegations began to surface. They resulted in Seoul Pabal, a club in the K-League's third tier, being closed down after several of its players were found guilty of being involved with a Chinese betting site in fixing results.

Three years later, 28-year-old Choi Sung-kuk, one of the biggest names in Korean football, was at the centre of a much bigger bribery scandal. His involvement was nothing short of sensational. Capped twenty-six times for his country – Choi was a member of South Korea's 2004 Olympic and 2007 Asian Cup teams – and with 200 domestic league games and thirty-one goals behind him, the winger who had been dubbed the 'Little Maradona' might have kept out of trouble if a proposed move to Sheffield United, who had just been relegated from the Premier League, had gone through. But it did not, Choi returned to his homeland and in December 2008 joined Gwangju Sangmu, a K-League club where younger players could fulfil their two years' compulsory military service. Released prior to the beginning of the 2011 season,

Choi signed a three-year contract for Suwon Samsung Bluewings and was appointed captain of his new club.

His career, however, was soon to come crashing down. In May 2011, he was named as one of the players implicated in the latest betting scandal. Choi was suspected of being involved in several fixed Gwangju Sangmu matches after being offered money – which he denied – by Sangmu player 28-year-old Kim Dong-hyun who had lured several younger players into the scam.

Kim was quite a piece of work. In May 2012, now broke and desperate following his suspension from football, along with a former baseball pitcher, Yoon Chan-su, he tried to kidnap a woman in an affluent area of Seoul. As she got out of her Mercedes at the underground car park of her home in the small hours of the morning, Kim threatened her with a knife. His intention was to collect a ransom but the woman managed to escape. Kim was sentenced to three years' imprisonment and five years' probation. He was yet another fine footballer – nicknamed 'Korea's Vieri', in 2002, he had led South Korea to victory in the Asian Under-20 Championships in Qatar – whose greed for easy money had ruined him.

Choi Sung-kuk and another player, Yoo Byung-soo of Incheon United, had protested their innocence before more than 1,000 people at a K-League 'workshop' held at the Hanwha Resort in Pyeongchang. On 31 May 2011, before an audience of players, coaches, referees and Korean Football Association (KFA) officials, Choi said that he had laughed when he first heard rumours that he had helped to fix matches. He said that he had always been focused on football and had never been involved in manipulating. 'If I had done anything wrong, I would've been summoned to the prosecution, and not here talking with you,' he said.

One month later, however, Choi took a different line about his alleged involvement in match-fixing. He told prosecutors that in June 2010, when he was playing for Gwangju Sangmu, he attended a meeting between players and representatives of a gambling syndicate. Despite his previous denial, he said that Kim Dong-hyun had indeed offered him money to help fix matches but that he had rejected it. Choi said that he had reported the incident to a Sangmu club official.

Choi's admission had come days after Yeom Dong-gyun, a goalkeeper with Jeonbuk Hyundai Motors, confirmed his own role in the affair as more players were identified as willing participants.

Lee Kap-jin, head of the KFA's newly-formed misconduct committee, told the Associated Press agency: 'We don't know how deep and wide it goes but I think it will take a long time to sort out. We only know what the prosecutors have found and the players who have come forward voluntarily to confess.'

Investigations continued, more names were implicated, and in 2012, the KFA placed lifetime suspensions on more than forty players who were banned from playing in any domestic competition. Choi Sung-kuk was one of them and when FIFA quickly extended the ban to apply worldwide, it put an end to any hopes that Choi entertained of immediately resuming his career in Macedonia with FK Rabotnički. In February 2012 he was also sentenced to a ten-month prison term, which was suspended for two years, and 200 hours of community service over the next ten months for his actions relating to match-fixing.

Twenty-one of the players, who had voluntarily admitted their offences, were placed on probation with the chance of returning to the game after between two and five years. Altogether more than sixty people, including those who brokered deals between players and gamblers, were indicted in rigging K-League matches. Eight of the players indicted were from the Daejeon Citizen club. One of them was alleged to have received the equivalent of £67,000, which he had shared among his teammates, to lose one match alone.

Besides banned players, professional football clubs themselves also suffered financially. The clubs received money from ticket sales of Sports Toto, the national sports lottery. Daejeon Citizen would now lose 30 per cent of its annual share. Gwangju FC and Sangju Sangmu Phoenix, which each had one player banned, would each lose 10 per cent of their lottery money.

In 2014, a reformed and wiser Choi Sung-Kuk joined the fight against match-fixing in South Korean football. After addressing the annual meeting of the International Federation of Professional Footballers in Tokyo, Choi, who had recently opened a Japanese izakaja-style restaurant in the city of Suwon in the north-west of South Korea, told the AFP news agency: 'For a lot of players, all they know is football – they aren't that intelligent ... If they are exposed, it's easy to fall into the same hole.' He said that he had attended the conference to help better educate young players in his home country so that they might understand the risks in the future.

> The most important thing is to protect and educate them so that they are aware of what's going on. There is probably a lack of knowledge. Players are not aware enough, so [betting syndicates] are able to penetrate and get close to the players.
>
> Most soccer players have only known soccer their entire lives, so when exposed to such temptations, they easily fall into it … We need to strengthen education for players to protect them from the temptation of match-fixing … Because players are not fully aware of the dangers of such temptation, they end up getting closer to match-fixing … I was suspended for five years, but I understand that punishment for such match-fixing must be severe and repeatedly emphasised. Maybe, though, it is also better to also give the players a choice, to re-educate them.

There were many casualties among those caught up in the scandal. Choi Sung-kuk was later pictured working as a hospital receptionist. A laudable job but so different from his previous glittering career as an international footballer. Far worse, however, were the fates of players who took their own lives. In May 2011, Yoon Ki-won, nine days short of his 24th birthday, was found dead in his car at a rest stop on an expressway near Seoul. Yoon had been first-choice for Incheon United at the start of the 2011 season but lost his place after a series of poor performances that belied his reputation as one of the K-League's best goalkeepers. His final game for Incheon was one of those in which You Byung-soo was implicated.

In April 2012, former Suwon Bluewings midfielder Lee Kyung-hwan, 24, was pronounced dead on his way to hospital after apparently jumping off the roof of his fifteen-storey apartment building in Incheon. Nine months earlier, Lee had been fined the equivalent of £4,250, ordered to undertake 300 hours of community service and banned for life by the KFA after being found guilty of deliberately making mistakes in matches when he was one of the eight Daejeon Citizen players accused of taking kickbacks to fix the outcome of matches.

The biggest shock of all was when Jung Jong-kwan was found hanged in a hotel room in Seoul in May 2011. The 30-year-old Jung was one of five players, along with two intermediaries, for whom arrest warrants had been issued several days earlier on suspicion of manipulating the results of matches. He had gone into hiding and then killed himself.

Until 2007 Jung – who had once been jailed for violating military service law and who, after being released, had continued to play professional football while doing public service as an alternative to the mandatory military service – had been playing for Jeonbuk Hyundai Motors in the K-League's top division, but more recently had been turning out for Seoul United in the third tier. His body had been discovered by a hotel employee, and there was no sign of forced entry into the room. Jung had left a written will, and a note beside his body read: 'I'm ashamed of myself as a person involved in the match fixing scandal. Those under investigation are all my friends and they haven't blown my name because of friendship. All is my fault and I got them involved.' One of the go-betweens arrested had played in the same school football team as Jung.

Five months after that grim discovery, Lee Soo-cheol, the head coach of K-League club Sangju Sangmu Phoenix, was found dead in yet another apparent suicide. The 45-year-old had been given a two-year suspended prison sentence with three years on probation after being found guilty blackmailing the parents of a young player connected to match-fixing. He had taken money from them in exchange for concealing the player's identity. According to local police, Lee had hanged himself in his home in Bundang, south of Seoul. 'No suicide note was found, but his family members said he has been distressed in recent months by the match-rigging scandal.'

After the 2011 scandal, Kwak Young-Cheol, head of the K-League's disciplinary committee, told journalists: 'We made the decision, determined that this would be the first and the last match-fixing scandal in the league.'

Alas, bribery continued to dog South Korean football. In 2015, the former CEO of Gyeongnam FC, Ahn Jung-buk, was found guilty of bribing referees to help his club avoid relegation. It worked for a season, but in 2014 Gyeongnam went down to K-League 2 after losing a relegation play-off.

In November 2018, the former international left-back Jang Hak-yong was banned for life by the KFA. Thirty-seven-year-old Jang, veteran of more than 300 domestic league and cup matches, had retired the previous year. In September 2018, Lee Han-saem, then a central defender with the military club Asan Mugunghwa, reported that Jang had offered him the equivalent of £35,000 if he got himself sent off within the first twenty minutes of a game against Busan IPark in the second division of the K-League that month. Lee refused and received from the KFA a reward that was bigger than the bribe offer. Jang was arrested and his reward was ten months' imprisonment.

Football was not the only sport in South Korea to suffer at the hands of unscrupulous gamblers and corrupt players and officials. In 2012, four volleyball players were banned for life, and in 2016 twenty-one people involved in the country's professional baseball league were charged. As recently as April 2023 the Korean Baseball Organisation asked prosecutors to look into allegations of illegal betting and improper contract negotiations.

Chapter 16

The Battle of Highbury

> It's a bit hard to play like a gentleman when somebody closely resembling an enthusiastic member of the Mafia is wiping his studs down your legs, or kicking you up in the air from behind.
>
> Eddie Hapgood, Arsenal and England

On 14 November 1934, no less than seven Arsenal players were in the England team that met World Cup holders Italy on the Gunners' Highbury home turf in front of a crowd of 56,000. The game was only one minute old when Arsenal's Ted Drake, who was making his full England debut, was fouled in the penalty area. Swedish referee Otto Olsson awarded a spot-kick but the normally reliable Eric Brook of Manchester City saw his shot magnificently saved by Carlo Ceresoli.

Brook soon atoned for his miss. In the seventh minute he headed England ahead from a free-kick taken by Everton's Cliff Britton, and four minutes later made it 2-0 with a 25-yard free-kick of his own. After twelve minutes Drake, who had been fouled, managed to stay on his feet long enough to find the back of the net and England were three goals ahead.

By then Italy were about to be reduced to ten men. Their centre-half, Luis Monti, had broken a small bone in his foot after Drake tackled him. It was not a vicious challenge and Monti tried to continue but could not and the Italians played the last seventy-three minutes a man down (no substitutes in those days). In the second half Italy pulled back to 3-2 through Giuseppe Meazza with goals in the fifty-eighth and sixty-second minute against Arsenal's goalkeeper Frank Moss, who was making the last of his five international appearances. But for the intervention of the woodwork the Italians might have equalised but that was how the game finished.

These are the simple match facts – but the match would be remembered for much more than that. It had long generated into violence as the Italians set out to disrupt England's football. This 'friendly' international would henceforth be known as the 'Battle of Highbury'.

Barely had the cheers for England's second goal died down when Arsenal's Eddie Hapgood, who that afternoon was captaining his country for the first time, was elbowed on the bridge of the nose by an Italian player. Hapgood returned to the action after the Arsenal and England trainer Tom Whittaker had patched him up with supports on either side of his nose, strapped on with sticking plaster.

Brook suffered a fractured arm – or was it a dislocated shoulder? Reports varied – and Drake was punched in the face. Two more Arsenal men were injured: Ray Bowden was kicked on the ankle; George Male, who was also making his debut, broke a bone in a hand. Nineteen-year-old Stoke City outside-right Stanley Matthews, playing in only his second full international, had sensed trouble almost from the kick-off. In his autobiography Matthews wrote that the crowd, 'who had paid good money to see a game of football were giving vent to their feelings … because they were witnessing a brawl'.

The *Daily Herald* reported: 'In the matter of injuries Eddie Hapgood was the worst sufferer … His nose had been broken, so one can truthfully say that the Arsenal left-back played a gallant game.'

The distinguished football writer W. Capel Kirby said that he had seen fiercely fought derby matches, and cup-ties of the 'veriest needle variety', but never had anything stirred him so much as this: 'English players were kicked, tripped, thrown down – yes – and even punched … the kicking, punching, wrestling and tripping continued until, in the end, it was a case of our players concentrating on wildly flying feet instead of the ball.'

There were those who pointed out that the Italians were robbed of Monti's services for almost all of the match, but 'against that, let me put it on record that in less than fifteen minutes of the start only two or three of our players had avoided getting the stuffing knocked out of them'.

> Somebody rolled on Eric Brook. A beautiful right hook landed flush on Ted Drake's left cheek. Bastin [another Arsenal player] was hooked up from behind, while Eddie Hapgood, left-full-back and captain, was led from the field

> his face hidden in a sponge. It had to be seen to be believed. The pity is that some of our players gave as good as they received.

Arsenal's 'hard man' Wilf Copping had certainly put himself about. According to Hapgood: 'For the first time in their lives the Italians were given a sample of real honest shoulder charging, and Wilf's famous double-footed tackle was causing them furiously to think.'

That evening Hapgood arrived at a dinner hosted for the teams by the Football Association with his nose stitched and heavily plastered, undeniable evidence of the sort of football match the international had turned into. An Italian official said that the players were very downhearted, especially over Monti's injury, while Ceresoli looked pale and was limping. The Italians' disappointment was probably as much to do with the fact that Benito Mussolini, Italy's dictator, who was being kept informed of the progress of the game as he worked at the Palazza Venezia, had promised each of them an Alfa Romeo car, together with the equivalent of £150 and exemption from their annual military service, if they beat England

Despite what had happened on the pitch a few hours earlier, the *Western Daily Press* reported that, although the teams sat at different tables, 'a pleasant spirit gradually pervaded the gathering'. Not quite. Hapgood had difficulty restraining himself when the Italian who had broken his nose laughed at him as he walked past the table at which his assailant sat.

Gifts were exchanged, a silver bowl for the Italian Football Association, and gold medals for its players, and a variety of gifts from the Italians to the English players. Referee Olsson received a gold watch. He said: 'The Italians are very excitable. When they learn how to control themselves they will be a great side. I had to warn two of the defenders repeatedly, but whether they understood me or not, I do not know. I hope that they did.'

W. Capel Kirby said that England were fighting for British prestige against a team boasting the title of world champions, and they did that 'most nobly and well'.

So British prestige was upheld, but people were asking: 'What is the point of sport if it is not to bring nations together?' The Sheffield *Daily Independent* held a firm view:

> International sport is supposed to promote international goodwill, or at least to exhibit the qualities of sportsmanship. The football match between England and Italy at Highbury yesterday has done neither. The best thing, therefore, is to stop these contests. There is enough discord in European affairs now without adding to it on the sports field. If there must be wrangling, let the politicians have a monopoly. It is absurd to try to stop political acerbities if we ought to have a different variety in the sporting world.

The *Manchester Evening News*'s special correspondent understood that the England-Italy game was 'likely to be the last of such matches for some years'.

> I believe that a strong attempt will be made by influential members of the Football Association to put an end to matches with Continental teams. The reason is that this was the roughest and ugliest looking representative match I have ever seen. It is felt by many big men in football that until the Italians in particular, and the Continental nations in general, change their outlook on these matches it will be better for England to keep out of them.

A member of the FA selection committee told the journalist:

> The match has left me and every member of the FA much distressed. I have watched football for many years in this and most of the countries, and I have never seen anything worse. The average spectator must have seen how flagrant were the fouls committed, but it was only the expert eye that could appreciate the outrage upon the sport. The FA is bound to consider the wisdom or otherwise of playing these matches.

The match had created huge interest in Italy where crowds gathered in the main squares to listen to a running commentary. 'An honourable defeat' was how the Italian press reported the game, and their overall view was that Italy would have won 'if they had not allowed themselves to be flustered at the start, and if Monti had been able to play for the full ninety minutes'.

As the Italian party left London on their way back home, their manager Commendatore Vittorio Pozzo – he had been awarded the honorary order of chivalry on the back of the World Cup success – said that they left 'with the warmest feelings' towards the England players and they hoped that a return match might be played the following year.

It would be May 1939 before the countries met again. With Europe hurtling towards the second world war in a generation, England began their summer tour with a match in the San Siro Stadium in Milan, where three days of heavy rain, a strong wind and a quagmire of a pitch quite suited them. The match was billed in Italy as 'the most important football match that has been played anywhere in the world since the Great War'.

To begin with, the Italians tried no Highbury-style rough stuff, and even when Everton's Tommy Lawton scored from a cross by Stanley Matthews after nineteen minutes they behaved themselves. Three minutes after half-time, Amedeo Biavati equalised, and after sixty-three minutes Italy went ahead with a controversial goal when Silvio Piola slipped on the greasy surface and back-handed the ball over his shoulder past Chelsea's Vic Woodley and into the net. For good measure Piola followed through and caught George Male a beauty over an eye.

After consulting a linesman the German referee, 'Peco' Bauwens, allowed the goal. Italy's Crown Prince Umberto offered to go down and order Bauwens to change his decision, a gesture politely declined by the FA secretary Stanley Rous, and with thirteen minutes remaining Tottenham's Willie Hall made it 2-2 when he beat the unsighted Aldo Olivieri. The star of England's performance, though, was Everton's Joe Mercer whose speed and awareness kept his team in the game during the first furious twenty minutes of the second half when the Italians resorted to the rough stuff. Stanley Matthews wrote: 'We were right back at Highbury, 14 November 1934.'

Tommy Lawton recalled: 'Had we been anybody other than Englishmen, there would have been a riot. But we'd come to expect it when we played Continentals. But we played in the proper spirit and afterwards the FA officials who had travelled with us thanked us privately for keeping our calm.'

At the after-match banquet an Italian official dwelt on the friendly relationship that the two countries enjoyed. A year later they were at war and battles of an entirely different kind lay ahead.

Chapter 17

The Battle of Santiago

> The World Cup is heading for ruin and disgrace unless Sir Stanley Rous, president of FIFA, and his committee act quickly to clean it up.
>
> Frank McGhee, *Daily Mirror*

It was a piece of film that had to be preceded by a warning from the BBC that it was not suitable for viewers of a nervous disposition. It was not a documentary from a war zone, although it might have been.

In June 1962, David Coleman introduced footage of the World Cup match played two days earlier between host nation Chile and Italy with the following words:

> The game you are about to see is the most stupid, appalling, disgusting and disgraceful exhibition of football in the history of the game. This is the first time these countries have met; we hope it will be the last. The national motto of Chile reads, 'By Reason or By Force'. Today, the Chileans weren't prepared to be reasonable, the Italians only used force, and the result was a disaster for the World Cup.

The World Cup has indeed seen a few black days in its near-100-year history, but 2 June 1962 ranks as perhaps its blackest. The Battle of Santiago would top the catalogue of shame that has all too often dogged football, and it was unfortunate that, thanks to television – the film still had to be flown around the world; no live streaming sixty-odd years ago – big matches were now being seen worldwide, and what viewers saw that night was Chileans and Italians serving up the ugliest side of football.

The 1962 tournament had been bedevilled long before the first ball was kicked. And when it finally did get under way, the early signs were not promising either. Bad fouls and sendings-off, in those early matches there was much to worry FIFA.

Chile had been awarded this World Cup in 1956 after back-to-back tournaments in Europe – Switzerland in 1954; Sweden in 1958 – had seen South American countries threaten a boycott if the tournament was not now returned to the Southern Hemisphere. Some powerful lobbying saw Chile selected ahead of Argentina, who had looked to be favourites. The Chilean Football Federation's president, Carlos Dittborn, promised: 'Because we have nothing we will do everything.'

Chile had to do 'everything' to continue to stage the tournament when, in May 1960, the Valdivia earthquake – at a magnitude of 9.5 the most powerful ever recorded in human history, killing more than 1,500 people, injuring thousands more and making 2 million homeless – dealt a huge blow to preparations for the World Cup two years later. Eight venues – Santiago, Viña del Mar, Rancagua, Arica, Talça, Concepción, Talcahuano and Valdivia – were planned but the number had to be reduced to four. Half the buildings in Valdivia alone were rendered uninhabitable.

There was more trouble ahead. As the opening of the tournament neared, two Italian journalists, Antonio Ghirelli of *Corriere della Sera* and Corrado Pizzinelli of *La Nazione*, began filing 'colour' pieces about the Chilean capital for their respective newspapers. They were certainly colourful; derogatory would be a better description.

Ghirelli said of Santiago: 'Has 700 beds (for visitors). The telephone doesn't work. Taxis are as rare as faithful husbands. A telegram to Europe is extremely expensive, an airmail letter takes at least five days.' Warming to his theme Ghirelli described the arrangements for the World Cup as:

> an impossible rendezvous with glory … Chile ought to realise that this championship must be faced like building a brick wall, wielding axe and trowel because people here … are used to earning their living by sweating blood.
>
> A world championship 13,000 kilometres [8,000 miles] away: pure madness. Chile is small, poor and proud. She undertook to organise this edition of the Rimet [World] Cup contest as Mussolini undertook to send our airplanes to bomb London (they didn't arrive) [actually 170 aircraft

from the Regia Aeronautica, Italy's Royal Air Force, took part in the Blitz].

Pizzinelli was equally scathing: 'Santiago is terrible. Entire neighbourhoods are given over to open prostitution,' while the Chilean people were described as likely to suffer from 'malnutrition, illiteracy, alcoholism and poverty'.

Articles sent back to Italy also claimed that the World Cup had been organised by Chile's ruling class as propaganda to support them in forthcoming elections and 'to give confidence to the Alliance for Progress' (a ten-year plan proposed by President John F. Kennedy in 1961 to foster economic cooperation between North and South America, particularly aimed at countering the perceived communist threat from Cuba).

Chileans were understandably angered by the Italians' claims and local reports said that, on the order of the minister of the interior, the international, political and emergency sections of the Santiago police force had been mobilised to expel Ghirelli and Pizzinelli. A police spokesman said that the charges were 'very grave', but that neither journalist had been found.

Other Italian reporters were quick to distance themselves from the opinions of the errant pair. A press conference was called to underline that the two were not part of the official Italian press delegation and that as far as everyone else was concerned, arrangements were 'perfect'.

The Chilean press hit back. *Clarín* headlined its article on the writings with 'World War', while *El Mercurio*, edited the articles to heighten the insults. Other newspapers described Italians in general as gangsters and drug addicts (only one month earlier, seven Serie A players from Inter Milan, Bologna and Mantova had tested positive during a drug test).

Back in Rome, *Corriere dello Sport* commented: 'It seems to us at this point that the campaign against our colleagues is distinctly exaggerated.' Passions were running high, however, and although Ghirelli and Pizzinelli managed to get out of the country unharmed, a few days before Italy were due to meet Chile in their second match of the tournament, an Argentinian journalist was severely beaten when he was mistaken for an Italian.

When the action finally began, the early signs were not good. In the eight games over the first two days, there were four sendings-off, three broken legs and a fractured ankle. The first match in England's group – Group Four – between Argentina and Bulgaria at the tiny ground belonging to the Braden Copper Company at Rancagua, near Valparaiso, attracted only 7,134 spectators who saw Spanish referee Juan Gardeazabal Garay awarded no less than sixty-nine free kicks. Bulgaria's Todor Diev came in for some particularly rough treatment as Argentina won 1-0 with a fourth-minute goal by Héctor Fecundo.

The USSR's opening match, against Yugoslavia, was something of a grudge match after the Soviets had beaten Yugoslavia to win the inaugural European Championship in Paris two years earlier. The USSR also won this game, 2-0, despite losing Eduard Dubinski to a heavy challenge by Muhamed Mujić that broke the Russian's leg. The Yugoslav was not sent off, but his association voluntarily suspended him for a year.

Italy's first match, against West Germany, was a bad-tempered goalless draw that kept Scottish referee Bobby Davidson busy and saw the Italians booed throughout by the majority of the 65,440 crowd, no doubt still seething at the literary efforts of Ghirelli and Pizzinelli. The *Daily Express* warned: 'The tournament shows every sign of developing into a violent bloodbath. Reports read like battlefront despatches; the Italy v West Germany match was described as "wrestling and warfare".'

Chile's opener saw them overcome an eighth-minute goal by Switzerland's Rolf Wüthrich to win 3-1. The match was refereed by England's Ken Aston. In 1940, Aston had refereed a game between the anti-aircraft site where he was stationed and a local RAF base. He recalled:

> We hear a low droning sound. It was a day of low cloud. We look up at the aircraft and it was a JU 88, a German light bomber. And so I raced to my gun, whipped on my steel helmet and respirator … and manned the guns in refereeing kit. We had to abandon the game.

Aston's next assignment at the 1962 World Cup was to take charge of Italy's game against Chile at the Estadio Nacional in Santiago. A steel helmet would have come in handy on that day, too. The first foul came within fifteen seconds of the kick-off; the first sending-off after eight minutes when Italy's Giorgio Ferrini was kicked from behind by Chile's centre-forward, Honorino Landa, who was the youngest player in the

Chilean squad; he had celebrated his twentieth birthday the previous day. Ferrini retaliated and Aston sent him off, but he refused to go. The game was held up for almost ten minutes before armed police escorted the Italian midfielder to the dressing-room.

The Italian players wanted to know why Landa had escaped without even a booking. The match further deteriorated as with heavy tackles and sharp elbows the Italians handed out as much as they received. When their captain, Humberto Maschio, fouled Chile's outside-left Leonel Sánchez, Sánchez, the son of a professional boxer, broke Maschio's nose with a classic left hook.

Remarkably, Sánchez, like Landa also escaped punishment. Emboldened by the let-off, he was soon at it again, this time punching Italy's right-half Mario David. Again the Chilean escaped without so much as a caution. As half-time approached, David decided that he had had enough and tackled Sánchez somewhere around his neck. Italy would play the second half with only nine men.

There was no justice to be had for Italy. In the seventy-fourth minute it was Sánchez who took the free-kick from which Jaime Ramírez gave Chile the lead. Two minutes from time, Jorge Toro made it 2-0. Italy were out, Chile were on their way to the quarter-finals and a 2-1 victory over the Soviet Union. That victory came on the day that the widow of Carlos Dittborn gave birth to a son. The Chilean Football Federation president had died shortly before the start of the World Cup that he had fought so hard to stage. His country went out in the semi-finals to Brazil, the eventual world champions, who won 4-2. There was yet more violence here and the teams ended up with ten men apiece. Landa was sent-off for a foul on Zito, and Garrincha was dismissed for kicking Rojas.

The tournament was over but the Battle of Santiago continued to be the main topic of conversation. Writing in *The Observer*, the Coventry City manager Jimmy Hill had summed up what many people were feeling:

> The Italians could not understand – and neither can I – why Sánchez had been allowed to remain on the field despite a passable imitation of Rocky Marciano, when one of their number had been banished for a less serious and far less obvious offence. From that moment the last semblance of control left both players and officials. It was an appalling

> decision to allow a player to remain on the field after such a blatant disregard for the laws. The players will have to shoulder most of the blame, but the officials must face up to their responsibility for making this grotesque decision.

Aston had his excuse:

> I had my back to the incident at the time. If the referee or linesman sees nothing, nothing can be done. I'm sure the linesman did see it, but he refused to tell me … I was stuck with a Mexican and a little American. They weren't very good, so it became almost me against the twenty-two players.

The American to whom Aston referred was Leo Goldstein, a Holocaust survivor who escaped the gas chamber when a Nazi guard asked if there was anyone who could referee a football match. Goldstein had never done so but quickly volunteered, survived the war, emigrated to the United States and continued to referee.

Aston said that it had crossed his mind to abandon the match, but, had he done so, then he could not have been responsible for the safety of the Italian players and, indeed, his own. He did, however, decide not to add any stoppage time. Immediately after the game, the Italian Football Federation cabled FIFA asking for 'the laws of hospitality to be respected' during the team's time in Chile and also demanding a 'full investigation' into Ken Aston's handling of the game. Aston had suffered an Achilles tendon injury and this would be his last World Cup match.

It was inevitable that there would be backlash against ex-patriot Italians living in Chile. Some restaurants and shops banned them, and one Italian restaurant proprietor said: 'After the Italian colony has been trying for forty years to create a good atmosphere, eleven types come and undo it all.'

There were arguments and counter-arguments. Dr Jorge Pica, president of the Chilean technical committee, issued a statement: 'It was abnormal. Now I can see the necessity for laboratory tests and a specialist to examine players after the game.' Pica, who was also a criminal court judge and at that time was handling a murder trial, told the newspaper *Clarín*: 'The Italians seemed to go on the field only with the intention of injuring the Chileans. It was like a rodeo. Frankly, I think they were doped.' FIFA had sought dope tests, but the Italians reportedly refused.

It was claimed that when Chile's medical officer, Dr Sergio Reyes, went into the Italian dressing room at half time he was spat at by Milan centre-half Sandro Salvadore.

Ireland's Harry Cavan, chairman of the World Cup appeals committee, said: 'It seems that the win-at-all-costs attitude of some of the teams is defeating the whole object of the tournament. Unless strong action is taken by referees, everything will get out of hand.'

Some referees hit back, criticising the World Cup organising committee for only cautioning one of the two Italian players sent off by Aston. Although Ferrini was suspended for one match, David received only a warning. After a report from the Yugoslavian FIFA official at the stadium, Leonel Sánchez was also cautioned. A previous World Cup rule had stipulated that when a player was sent off he was automatically suspended for the rest of the tournament, but this was amended for the 1962 competition. FIFA president Sir Stanley Rous said: 'We can only hope the punishments we have announced will prove effective.'

FIFA's press statement did not mention Chilean allegations that the Italians had been doped, but after the committee's two-and-a-half-hour hour meeting a warning was issued to trainers, coaches, officials and players. They were told that FIFA would take action against delegates of countries as a whole if there were any further breaches of rules. The *Belfast Telegraph*'s Malcolm Brodie commented: 'I assume this means that if officials cannot make their teams behave properly, the nation involved could be expelled from the current series or even future championships.'

Addressing a special meeting of the World Cup organising committee and representatives of some of the competing nations, Rous said that 'the brawling has got to stop'. He said that television films of the World Cup matches would show the game in a very bad light when seen by the rest of the world, and he added that the competition had got to be finished in better fashion than it had been started.

> Already certain parties are talking about changing the form of the competition, but that would be a grave mistake. East must meet West, and Europe must meet South America in order to prove to players and spectators alike that the game

> is played under the same rules and conditions. We had no such trouble in Switzerland, Sweden and Brazil. What has happened?

Recalling his opening address to the competing nations, when he told them that good sportsmanship was expected, Rous said: 'I was too optimistic.' When Rous said that what had been seen so far was not unusual in South America, the Chilean president of the finals, Juan Goni, interrupted: 'FIFA has been misinformed. It is not the habit to play rudely here.' Sepp Herberger, the West German manager, promised that his team would play 'kid-gloves football'.

In Rome, deputies of the neo-fascist party Movimento Sociale Italiano (Italian Social Movement) tabled a parliamentary motion asking what steps the Italian government was taking to protest at the inhospitable treatment of the Italian team at the World Cup. The motion referred to a campaign of 'hostility, intimidation and violence' against Italian footballers and journalists in Chile. In a debate in the Chamber of Deputies, a Communist deputy went so far as to criticise Ken Aston. Of the Chile players he said they 'were not athletes of the twentieth century but gladiators of the imperial epoch'. Additional police were stationed around the Chilean embassy in the fashionable Parioli quarter of the Italian capital to prevent possible demonstrations. Embassy officials said that after the game was shown on Italian television the previous evening, numerous menacing telephone calls had been received.

The Santiago edition of the daily newspaper *El Mercurio* said: 'The Italians decided to send a boxing team,' and Swiss football writers describe themselves as 'war correspondents filing dispatches from the Santiago front'.

In the *Daily Herald*, Peter Lorenzo wrote:

> These 1962 World Cup finals will become soccer's most shameful saga of savagery unless FIFA president Sir Stanley Rous and his organising committee step in and get tough NOW before it is too late. In the first twelve matches, thirty-seven players have been injured. Five for being sent off. Referees threatened to strike unless they are given stronger backing after they've ordered players off.

> Switzerland say they will not compete again unless there is a clean-up.
>
> World champions Brazil with the great Pelé injured against Czechoslovakia and out of the game for a week, write a letter of protest against dirty play.
>
> But the sickening story of spine-chilling tackling, explosive tempers and bar-room thuggery which are making nonsense of the meaning of the word sport will go disgracefully on unless Sir Stanley, world soccer leader, can stop it.

One referee told Lorenzo: 'We don't get any match fees, just hotel and travel expenses. We're here just for the ride, but not to be taken for a ride.'

Chapter 18

The Battle of Montevideo

> The worst victim was football. One of the world's major trophy games became a back-street brawl.
>
> Roger Baillie,
> *Sunday Mirror.*

From glory to shame, and all inside six months. On the balmy evening of 25 May 1967, in the Estádio Nacional in Lisbon, Scottish League champions Celtic, their players all born within a twenty-five-mile radius of Glasgow, became the first British club to win the European Cup. 'We did it by playing football. Pure, beautiful, inventive football,' Celtic's manager Jock Stein told the waiting press.

On 4 November 1967, in the Estadio Centenario in Montevideo, Celtic played in a world club championship play-off – the Intercontinental Cup to give it its official name – against the champions of South America, Racing Club of Argentina. Afterwards Stein declared: 'I would not bring a team to South America again for all the money in the world.'

The fixture was intended to be played over two legs to find the winner on aggregate. It led to one of the most infamous football matches in the history of the game. After Celtic won 1-0 at Hampden Park, and Racing triumphed 2-1 at the El Cilindro de Avellaneda in greater Buenos Aries, the tie went to a play-off in 'neutral' Uruguay. It would be forever known as the Battle of Montevideo.

The fixture had already aroused plenty of controversy. In front of 83,437 fans at Hampden Park, Billy McNeill's sixty-ninth-minute header had settled the first leg and Racing's players were accused of cynical fouls and spitting at their opponents. At one point, Juan Carlos Rulli upended Jimmy Johnstone and for the second time in the match Spanish referee Juan Gardeazábal was surrounded by angry Celtic players. A linesman had to come on to help clear the melee.

Afterwards, Stein said that every Celtic player had needed treatment for injuries, and Bobby Lennox was so badly hurt that he was ruled out of Scotland's Home International match against Northern Ireland in Belfast that weekend.

Newspaper reaction was varied. 'Ruthless Argentinians Are Defeated,' was the headline in *The Scotsman*. The *Aberdeen Press and Journal* said:

> The Racing Club technique and tactics included tripping, pushing and jersey-pulling in their efforts to stifle the inventive genius of the Parkhead forwards. Their tactics all but succeeded and they certainly detracted from the entertainment value of the game. Spanish referee Juan Gardeazábal failed to discipline the players who stepped out of line. He was much too tolerant.

The French newspaper *L'Equipe* said that Celtic had 'dominated their rivals territorially' and won in 'extremely difficult circumstances', in 'a furious battle' marred by too many fouls. Spain's sport newspaper *Marca* praised Racing's defence against such a dominant Celtic side, but Italy's *La Gazetta Dello Sport* countered that Celtic were lucky to win and that the Scots 'did not enchant anyone'.

The second leg was not even under way when Celtic were forced to change their goalkeeper after Ronnie Simpson was struck on the head by an object thrown from the crowd. John Fallon was called up as Celtic's trainer, Neil Mochan, led a dazed Simpson off the pitch which was now a milling mass of photographers and broadcast journalists hoping to talk to the players as they went through the usual pre-match kick-in routines.

Celtic might have taken the lead after only three minutes, but Stevie Chalmers saw his header brilliantly saved by Agustín Cejas. After twenty-two minutes they did go ahead, from a Tommy Gemmell penalty after Johnstone was brought down. Gemmell put the ball in the net despite the efforts of Argentinian press photographers who did their best to distract him, even going on to the pitch to gesticulate at him. Twelve minutes later, however, Racing equalised with a brilliant looping short-range header from Norberto Raffo.

Simpson watched the second half from the bench, his head wrapped in bandages and a towel, and three minutes after the interval he saw Racing take the lead through Juan Carlos Cárdenas, who was put clear through by Rulli and scored easily.

Uruguayan referee Esteban Marino, more familiar with Argentinian footballers' antics than was Senor Gardeazábal in the first leg, managed to keep a lid on further violence, although Celtic were not all that pleased with the official, claiming that they had had one good goal disallowed and should have had two more penalties.

With no further score, the aggregate stood at 2-2 and Celtic faced a play-off in Montevideo three days later. According to many accounts, no one in the Celtic camp was looking forward to it and the players wanted to return home immediately. Bobby Lennox, however, wrote later that, after the final whistle in Buenos Aries, Celtic's chairman, Bob Kelly, went into the dressing room and announced: 'That's it. We fly home tomorrow.' Said Lennox: 'But Jock knew the mood of the players. Despite being kicked by them for two matches, we still felt we could win the tie and eventually got our way.'

Stein told reporters: 'We don't want to go to Montevideo or anywhere else in South America for a third game. But we know we must.' He said that he was 'astonished' at Racing's behaviour: 'They did not need to do it. They were the better players today and won fairly. Look at my boys. This is not football. As far as I am concerned we are ready to fly home at any time. In my opinion the play-off is in very grave doubt.'

Stein demanded as assurance of better security and pointed out that a 4ft-high fence, a steel barrier and 900 policemen could not keep his players safe – witness Ronnie Simpson being assaulted even before the game had kicked-off.

Some Celtic players later said that although they were ready to go home, Stein was the one who wanted to settle the issue. Whatever, the team flew to Buenos Aries. And what awaited them was even worse than they had feared.

After twenty-three minutes of the play-off, Paraguayan referee Rodolfo Pérez Osorio stopped the action and called the captains together to warn them that if the persistent fouling by both teams did not stop, then players would be sent off. Seventeen minutes later, Alfio Basile and Bobby Lennox were the first to go. Juan Carlos Rulli had already tripped Jimmy Johnstone on the edge of the penalty area. Then Rulli hacked at Johnstone again. It was a savage foul and referee Osorio found himself again surrounded by protesting Scots. A brawl broke out and steel-helmeted policemen raced on to the pitch, one of whom had to be helped off, bleeding from face. Basile, who Lennox had accused of spitting at him in an earlier incident, was dismissed, and Lennox followed, although he had been simply a bystander. Stein ordered Lennox to return to the pitch. Osorio spotted him and sent him off again. Basile had already protested that he was a victim of mistaken identity. Rulli, whose foul on Johnstone had started the trouble, escaped without even having his name taken. It was a farce.

There was now no going back from the thuggery. Three minutes into the second half, Johnstone was elbowed by Racing's captain, Oscar Martín. A punch was thrown and Johnstone joined Lennox in the Celtic dressing-room. One could have sympathy for the fiery little redhead who had been a target for Racing's defenders throughout the first two matches and now this one. He could at least add one more achievement to his curriculum vitae: the first Scottish player to be sent off while already being suspended; a twenty-one day domestic ban on him had been lifted by the Scottish FA so that he could play against Racing.

In a rare moment of football, Cárdenas scored the fifty-fifth-minute goal that brought Racing their first world club title and the fifth in the competition's eight-year history for a South American club. Cárdenas's shot from just outside the penalty area gave John Fallon no chance.

Despite being down to nine men, Celtic twice came close to equalising when Willie Wallace saw first his shot saved and then his header flash inches wide of a goalpost. But with fifteen minutes remaining the Scots lost another player when John Hughes was sent-off for aiming a kick at Agustín Cejas (he could have been attempting to knock the ball out of the goalkeeper's hands), who collapsed dramatically.

Bobby Murdoch might have been the next to be banished after he decided that Raffo was faking an injury and dragged him over the touchline. Luckily for Murdoch, referee Osorio had long ago lost control and the Scot escaped censure.

Rulli was the last to go after he fouled Tommy Gemmell. Celtic's Bobby Auld denied that he had been sent off as Osorio claimed. The referee was quoted in the Montevideo press as saying that he ordered off the veteran Auld two minutes from the end in a scuffle broken up by Uruguayan policemen. 'I know nothing about it,' Auld told journalists.

John Blair, who was covering the game for *The People*, said that the longer the game had gone on the more violent it had become: 'If half-an-hour's extra-time had been necessary we might have had the fantastic situation of finishing six-a-side.'

Blair said that he had witnessed punch-ups in all parts of Europe, but nothing as shameful as what had just happened in Montevideo.

> From the first ball, two things were evident … The referee was weak and Racing were in a 'win at all costs' mood. And it's regrettable that Celtic, who have gloried in their football skills over the past year, should have descended to the Argentinian level before the end.

As the players strolled in small groups near their hotel in Montevideo, awaiting an evening flight home, Tommy Gemmell summed up the general feeling: 'We're all disillusioned by the result and the brutality of yesterday's match.' Meanwhile, Jimmy Johnstone, one of the five players sent-off – had 'never seen such bad refereeing in my life' – returned to the scene of the battle to fulfil a promise to play in a benefit match for the Uruguayan footballers' union.

Roger Baillie, reporting from Montevideo for the *Sunday Mirror*, said that the match reached a stage where 'you wondered whether each tackle would end in a brawl'. The Uruguayan press was unanimous in its condemnation of players' behaviour. *La Mañana* said: 'We witnessed a reign of indiscipline, of treachery and of impropriety driven to its maximum expression.' Under the headline, 'Oh, Football. Sorry,' *El Pais* said that a 'defrauded public' had been innocent victims of a disgusting display. *El Dia* called it a game of 'deplorable excesses', and *El Popular* described the 'lamentable spectacle' as 'a final which our football fans did not deserve'. Argentinean commentators were, understandably, quick to point the blame at one club. They recalled Jock Stein's comments after the match in Buenos Aries when he said that, while Celtic players would not look for trouble, they would give 'as much as they are forced to take'. The home media also highlighted Stein's comments to journalists that Celtic wanted to win the title, not so much for themselves but 'to stop Racing from becoming world champions'.

FIFA's president, Sir Stanley Rous, said: 'FIFA is bound to take some action in this rather complicated and disturbing matter when we receive the reports of the referee, the clubs and the football associations concerned.' It was a view at odds with what Sir Stanley had said after Ronnie Simpson had been unable to play in the second-leg match in Buenos Aries. Then he thought that FIFA would be unlikely to take action because it regarded the matches between the European Cup winners and the winners of the South American equivalent to decide the world club champions as 'a friendly fixture'.

The *Belfast Telegraph* correspondent wondered whether a British team would ever again compete in a world club championship fixture: 'The image of the competition was cast into deep shadow after universal condemnation of a brawling, foul-infested title play off.'

Twenty-four hours after the Battle of Montevideo, the Battle of Vienna erupted when violence broke out at the European Championship match between Austria and Greece in the Prater Stadium. More than 200 police officers went on to the pitch to break up fights between spectators and players when sections of the 32,000-strong crowd invaded the playing area four minutes from time after Hungarian referee Gyula Gere had sent off Greece's star player Takis Loukanidis.

It was a bad-tempered match scarred by a succession of heavy fouls, yet as far as the European Championship was concerned this last Group Three fixture was inconsequential as the Soviet Union had already claimed the only qualifying place. When Loukanidis, a living Greek god to many fans, was dismissed there was unrest on the terraces, and when another Greek player, Aristidis 'Kamaras' Katrodaylis, was warned for fouling an opponent it was the signal for a pitch invasion. Hordes of away supporters made for Gere, who was hit on the head with an empty bottle. A full-scale riot was now under way as Austrian police, both mounted and on foot – some with dogs, all of them wielding long sticks – battled to clear the pitch.

The match was abandoned and, as Mr Gere waited in his dressing-room before being taken to hospital, some 2,000 fans rampaged around the stadium chanting his name. The 1-1 scoreline stood, and UEFA threatened Austria with having to play all matches away from home if such an incident happened again.

The Austrian FA president, Hans Walch, said: 'It was a sad day for me. Nothing like this has happened in my eleven years as president.' Greece's manager, Lakis Petropolous, said: 'Up to the last twenty minutes the game was well played. What happened in the last fifteen had nothing to do with football. Fanaticism among spectators is alright but it should not get out of hand.'

Football rowdyism was not confined to matches abroad that weekend. Fifty spectators had been ejected at White Hart Lane during the Spurs-Liverpool match. A senior Metropolitan Police officer described the disturbance as 'no more than usual'.

Chapter 19

The Shame of Heysel

> It was gruesomely symbolic that television cameras should show a huge back-and-white Juventus flag being used as a shroud for bodies piled on the Brussels terraces. Those corpses utter for all of us, for the good of what is left of our football.
>
> Leon Hickman, *Birmingham Mail*

On Sunday, 29 October 2023, the bus carrying Olympique Lyonnais players and officials towards the Stade Velodrome in Marseille for a Ligue 1 match against Olympique Marseille was attacked by followers of the home team. Missiles – rocks and other projectiles – were thrown at the vehicle which resulted in Lyon's head coach, Fabio Grosso, suffering serious facial injuries that almost led to him losing the sight of an eye. To add insult to injury, one month later Grosso was sacked after his seven games in charge had resulted in only one win.

Nine people were arrested, the game was postponed and Olympique Marseille issued a statement which read: 'The club wishes a speedy recovery to Lyon coach Fabio Grosso and strongly condemns this violent behaviour which has no place in the world of football and in society.'

Hooliganism has long been a part of football. After an FA Cup match at Villa Park in February 1910, drunken Derby County supporters rampaged through the streets of Birmingham after their team had lost 6-1. One Colonel Ludlow wrote to a Birmingham newspaper: 'They are utterly indisciplined and the result of this lack of discipline on Saturday was the death of one of these poor misguided enthusiasts who lost his life under the wheels of a train at New Street station.'

The dead man was Joseph Scattergood, a 44-year-old Derbyshire coalminer who had fallen on to the line after being pushed forward on a crowded platform. The coroner, Mr I. Bradley, said that it was extremely sad that a man who had gone out to watch a football match with his son should meet with such a fearful accident.

Over the decades, football supporters would die in disorder at football matches all over the world. Instances were relatively rare, but when they occurred they scarred the game. None more so than in May 1964, at the Estadio Nacional in Lima, where more than 300 fans were killed after violence erupted at a Peru v Argentina game.

The prize at stake was a place in that year's Olympic Games in Tokyo. In the dying minutes of the game the referee disallowed an equalising goal for the home team. Two fans ran on to the pitch. One of them, a well-known local bouncer, attempted to strike the referee, and both interlopers were brutally assaulted by police.

That sparked a much bigger pitch invasion by fans angered at what they were seeing. In an attempt to prevent further encroachment on to the playing area, police fired tear gas into sections of the 53,000 crowd. Spectators panicked, there was a mass stampede down several flights of stairs for the exits – which were closed by shutters made from corrugated steel. Eventually the weight from the crush of fleeing fans was enough to burst open the shutters. But for many it was too late. The overwhelming majority of the estimated 328 that died – the exact number has never been established – did so from asphyxia or internal haemorrhaging. In the streets a running battle began between police and fans, and shots were fired. A judge ruled that anyone killed by gunfire outside the stadium would not be included in the official count of fatalities. It was the most appalling tragedy.

There are, of course, other names that are burned deeply into football's scroll of shame. None more so than Heysel.

On 29 May 1985, Liverpool and Juventus supporters travelled in their thousands to Brussels for the European Cup Final. The Merseyside club were seeking to lift the trophy for the fourth time, and for the second time in succession. Twelve months earlier, Liverpool had beaten AS Roma on penalties in the Stadio Olimpico in the Eternal City. Before, during and after the match Liverpool fans were subjected to harassment and violence. There were many tales of beatings and stabbings. Police largely ignored what was happening. Some fans sought refuge in the British Embassy.

There was, however, much worse to come. Twelve months later English and Italian fans occupied opposite end of the crumbling Heysel Stadium before an intended neutral section next to Liverpool's end began to fill up with Juventus supporters who had bought tickets on the day, from touts, from locals who had decided to cash in, even from the stadium ticket office itself. What happened next is open to debate. The only certainty is that thirty-nine people would die in the Heysel Stadium that evening and more than 400 would be injured. Those deaths occurred before the match had started, but it was decided that the game should still go ahead. That Juventus won 1-0 with a fifty-eighth-minute penalty from Michel Platini now seems utterly inconsequential. Heysel will be forever remembered for what happened before a ball was kicked.

About an hour before the scheduled kick-off, Liverpool fans broke down the flimsy fence between them and the neutral section that now contained mostly Juventus supporters. When the majority of the Italians fled, they found themselves trapped by a concrete retaining wall. Eventually this collapsed. Thirty-two Italians were killed, along with four Belgians, two French and a young man from Northern Ireland.

Hours before the game, Liverpool's manager, 64-year-old Joe Fagan, had announced his retirement. 'I'm relinquishing my post by mutual agreement,' said Fagan, who had taken over from Bob Paisley two years earlier. 'There are two reasons for my decision. The first is that I'm too old and the second is that I'm a little bit tired. It needs a younger man.' After Heysel, Fagan said that he was not sorry to be turning his back on the game he had loved so much.

Michel Platini, the man who scored the winning goal, reflected: 'The match should not have gone ahead. Tonight, despite our victory, I am a sad man. For football I am heartsick.' France's Michel Hidalgo, one of Europe's leading coaches, was also sad: 'This is the defeat of soccer. The end of the European Cup. We are all guilty.'

The blame, however, was laid firmly on Liverpool supporters. Some told of their horror as they watched their fellow fans start the trouble. Paul Fry, a freelance journalist from Stevenage, said that the trouble began when a large group of Liverpool fans set off flares and chanted taunts at the adjoining enclosure where Juventus supporters were congregated.

> The Juventus fans got angry, then the Liverpool ones reacted by throwing missiles – lumps of concrete the size of your hand, anything. They started wielding metal bars and chasing the Juventus fans. Then they ripped down the fence between them and spilled over and caused all that damage.

Jim Montgomery, who had attended Liverpool's four previous European Cup wins, threw his banner, scarf and hat into a gutter when he heard of the death toll:

> A group of six of us were in Section Z of the stadium and there's no doubt the Liverpool fans started the trouble. I saw a young Italian girl – she couldn't have been more than 15, the same age as my son – stuck on the top of the safety fence dripping in blood. Do you know what the bastards did? They tried to 'help' her over the fence by chucking bricks at her. That's the end for me. I'll still go to the games at Anfield but I'll never wear Liverpool's colours outside the city again.

Giuseppe Gola, an Italian businessmen from Verona, said that a policeman opened a door in the fencing that allowed more Liverpool supporters who were pressing against it to rush into the already crowded Juventus enclosure where fans included women and children.

Eyewitnesses said there were just a handful of police on duty – only twelve officers according to one account – at the spot where the violence broke out and they did nothing to prevent the charge that led to the fatal crush. The overcrowding caused the crowd to spill forward on to the 3ft-high wall fronting the running track surrounding the pitch. The wall broke under the pressure. Some supporters escaped on to the track but many others were crushed by the wall or trampled to death.

'It was butchery. I've never seen anything like it,' said Lorenzo Vassano, a teenage Juventus supporter. Another fan told journalists: 'Football is over for ever after tonight. I have seen death from too close.'

Alan Parker, from Ware in Hertfordshire, had supported Liverpool for years. He had a ticket for the ill-fated Z block. He arrived about twenty minutes late and as he was about to enter the stadium he saw fleeing Italian fans jumping over the wall. He told the *Hertford Mercury and Reformer*:

> It was absolute mayhem. It was so terrifying seeing little old ladies with blood all over their faces. We didn't know – and half the people in the ground didn't know at the time – what

> had happened. As we were walking away we saw a whole lot of Juventus fans coming running out of the ground. The organisation was diabolical. There was no police outside the ground. Whoever cut down the allocation of tickets to Liverpool fans and sold tickets to Juventus supporters should be held responsible.

Two housewives told the *Walsall Observer* how they helped injured and dying Juventus fans after they themselves had been dragged to safety through a hole in the stadium wall. Together with schoolteacher Ian Weaver, Irene Henderson and Beryl Clayton had travelled to Brussels with members of the West Midlands branch of the Liverpool Supporters Club.

Mrs Clayton, who was from Wallasey, said:

> We could feel something was going to erupt. We managed to squeeze our way to the back of the terrace where some lads had kicked a hole in the wall to get in. We were on our knees, shouting to the riot police and they dragged us out by our feet. Then, about ten seconds later, we heard a bang as the other wall collapsed. It was absolutely terrible, people being carried out dead and injured. We tried to help, using tissues to wipe blood from the faces of some of the injured, and trying to comfort others. An Italian man came out carrying his injured son. People were sobbing, and we could feel the bitterness. One man glared at us and made a sign across his throat to suggest we all needed killing.

Mrs Henderson said: 'We realised how lucky we were to get out. We did not stay to see the match after that. I was frightened and just sat on the coach.'

Ian Weaver said: 'There was a loutish political element there, out to make trouble. It was a minority of scum which the "sheep" followed. But crowd control was shocking. People in our coach got into the match without anyone taking their tickets off them.'

Gerald Bickley, the assistant secretary and treasurer of the supporters' club branch, said:

> When we got back to Ostend after the game the police advised us to stay in the hotel for our own safety because feelings were so high. What happened in that stadium was horrific, sickening. At the moment I feel I never want to go to another football match. We all felt so ashamed.

One Liverpool fan wrote to Prime Minister Margaret Thatcher to tell her that the cause of the violence was the beating dealt to a prone Liverpool fan by Juventus supporters. Twenty-year-old Mark Griffiths said that he wanted to 'put the record straight' as he felt that most accounts had been misleading and biased. He said that it was only after about twenty Liverpool fans had broken through a barrier to rescue their terrified colleague that more than 100 Juventus fans attacked the rescue mission. It was then that 'all hell broke loose', when Italians surged forward and the wall collapsed leading to most of the deaths.

Another Liverpool fan, 34-year-old sales representative Chris Jeffries of Kidsgrove, told Mrs Thatcher:

> I condemn as disgusting and sickening the actions of the scum who have dragged my country's name through the mud, but urge you as a person of truth and justice to see that any inquiry finds the truth not only about the British and Italian thugs but also brings UEFA and the Belgian police force to task for their part in the massacre.

He said that 'the inaction of the Belgian police was nothing short of cowardice and criminal negligence'. He also said that after an initial charge by British fans, some thirty minutes elapsed when rioting, fighting and missile throwing continued with only slight intervention from the police. 'This was before the Italians piled on to the pitch which meant that the disaster could have been avoided.'

There were several heroes among the Liverpool fans, however, and one of them, 27-year-old part-time barman John Welsh, told the *Liverpool Echo*'s Andy Byrne that he had gone to the match with his uncle.

> We walked into the stadium and found ourselves in a riot. I threw away my flag and dived into the crowd to help.

> I managed to get one young girl on the pitch and hand her over to a medic. I went back and that's when the wall collapsed on top of me. But I managed to get away and drag another man clear. He was choking to death and as I tried to free his tongue he almost bit my finger off.

He rescued a 19-year-old Italian girl:

> I went back into the crush but people were underneath me, grabbing my legs, and I got scared. I started going backwards towards the pitch and realised I was trampling over the dead. I went in the ambulance to the hospital with the last girl I got out. She was holding a thin wedding ring and trying to tell me something but I couldn't understand it. It was the saddest moment of my life when she died.

In Italy eight survivors that John Welsh managed to save said they owed their lives 'to the angel Liverpool fan in the pale yellow jumper'. Juventus fan 27-year-old Guiseppe Gallegari wanted to meet his English saviour. He told *La Gazette dello Sport*:

> We owe our lives to this Liverpool supporter. He is the one in the picture pulling an Italian to safety. Immediately afterwards, he dragged me out when I was powerless to move and getting suffocated. I would so much like to meet him and thank him personally for saving my life.

Newspapers now began to look back at Britain's grim catalogue of violence at football matches abroad. Thirteen years earlier, Glasgow Rangers had been suspended from European football after their supporters rioted in Barcelona.

In 1975, Leeds United were banned from European competition for four seasons after their fans ran amok during the European Cup Final against Bayern Munich in Paris.

In 1980, the FA was fined £8,000 after England fans caused trouble in Turin during a European Championship match against Belgium.

In 1981, English fans caused £60,000 worth of damage in Basle after a World Cup defeat by Switzerland. Sixteen spectators were injured.

There were fifty-nine arrests when English fans again rioted after another World Cup defeat, this time by Norway in Oslo. There were twenty arrests and one policeman was knocked unconscious.

In 1984, a Tottenham Hotspur fan was shot dead on the eve of the club's UEFA Cup Final first leg against Anderlecht after a row in a bar in the red light district of Brussels. The bar owner was charged with his murder. Two hundred Spurs' fans were arrested before and after the match when they rampaged through the streets of the Belgian capital.

There had been trouble on Brussels terraces before. In 1982 when trouble flared behind one goal at the Anderlecht-Aston Villa European Cup semi-final, it was Villa's own club stewards who attempted to restore order between rivals supporters after the local police withdrew.

The *Birmingham Mail*'s Leon Hickman recalled that Villa made a number of submissions to UEFA.

> These included: broken UEFA rules on crowd-control, tickets on sale immediately before the match, fans allowed in opposition areas, inadequate barriers, poor policing and deliberate provocation of the sort that was displayed on a 'Red Animals' banner last night.
>
> Eye witness accounts from the Heysel Stadium supported commentators' opinions that the police and organiser bothered insufficiently with a number of matters. The portable barriers were derisively impractical as a means of segregation and, even worse, it appears that fans in the area of the slaughter were mixed. Today, however, is not a day for inquests. It is for mourning. Tomorrow the inert body beneath a shroud may be football's – certainly as a pleasurable entertainment.

A British engineer told the magazine *New Civil Engineer* that although Liverpool fans had triggered the disaster, the outdated and 'appallingly badly maintained' Heysel ground was the mechanism. He said that the arena broke all European soccer safety rules and should not have staged the match. He discovered badly crumbling concrete posts and rusted reinforcements throughout the terraces. The ground would not have received a safety certificate in Britain. He said that the crush barriers and fences were unsafe and the stadium would never have passed the

Safety of Sports Grounds Act. It would have been closed immediately. Jan Korff, deputy structural engineer of the Greater London Council, added that he believed the main killer at Heysel was the crush barriers. Along with London Fire Brigade's deputy chief officer, Gerry Clarkson, he made his investigation on the day following the disaster, when he also noticed an absence of 'reasonable means of escape'. The only exit gate in the vicinity was apparently locked.

In April 1989, after a five-month trial, fourteen of the twenty-six Liverpool supporters charged were found guilty of assault and battery that resulted in involuntary manslaughter. They were each sentenced to three years' imprisonment; half of each sentence was suspended. They had already spent six months in gaol on remand and all fourteen were allowed to leave Belgium immediately and given leave to appeal.

Albert Roosens, the former secretary-general of the Royal Belgian Football Association, who was accused of careless handling of the ticket sales for the game, received a nine-month suspended sentence.

Two senior police officers faced trials. Captain Johan Mahieu, who was responsible for the organisation of the police presence at the stadium on the evening, also received a nine-month suspended sentence after being found guilty of having failed to take necessary precautions. Major Michel Kensier, who had overall responsibility for the maintenance of order from the gendarmerie's headquarters, was acquitted in a civil action brought by families of the dead.

UEFA banned all English clubs from competing in European competitions for five years. Liverpool's ban was first set at ten years and later reduced to six. Long before the game, Liverpool's club secretary had asked UEFA to consider carefully the wisdom of 'staging the European Cup Final in a stadium that was due for demolition'. UEFA's president, Jacques Georges, and its general secretary, Hans Bangerter, were ultimately given conditional discharges by the court. Bangerter said: 'We have reached the stage now where football is at the crossroads. We cannot and are not willing to let this game be killed by irresponsible elements who have no place in football stadiums.' But he also criticised the police:

> The [Heysel] disaster would not have happened if our specific instructions on security had not been so badly disregarded by the Brussels police and especially the

> gendarmerie. The English vandals would not have been able to perform such terrible deeds and create such misery if they had not been helped by the frightful incompetence of the Belgian security forces.

A Belgian television broadcaster said that it had 'absolutely reliable' information that as the rioting was brought under control, it was thought best to rig the result in favour of Juventus. Hans Bangerter said that the allegation was 'incredible, absolutely ridiculous', and threatened to sue the TV station

But was there an even darker element than a crumbling stadium, poor administration and incompetent policing to the Heysel tragedy? Liverpool's chairman, John Smith, said that after he returned home from Belgium he was confronted by six National Front members. He said that they were delighted with the death and destruction in the Heysel Stadium. 'The National Front were there. I saw them. Six of them came up to me. I'm not prepared to say what they said, but they announced themselves and mentioned Chelsea Football Club.'

Returning Liverpool supporters also spoke of seeing National Front leaflets being handed out before the start of the game. A party of forty-eight supporters from Southport said leaflets bearing National Front logos were given out by young men draped in Union Flags and wearing Liverpool supporters' scarves and hats. They said the men spoke with 'Cockney' accents.

Liverpool claims of National Front involvement in the Heysel disaster were backed up by lecturer David Capitanchik, who had studied the role of extremist groups. Capitanchik, said that there was no doubt that members of the National Front distributed their literature at football matches and tried to recruit members from the crowds.

'I don't know if the National Front is capable of organising something like the riot in Brussels,' he said, but he felt that it was possible that such violence might have been organised by such groups.

There was evidence that Italian fans had also made preparations for the game with printed banners containing abusive slogans, and that weapons had been taken into the ground. Capitanchik pointed out that Italy also had its extremist groups similar to the National Front.

Eight days after Heysel, when England met Italy at the Stadio Azteca in Mexico, the English players wore black armbands as a mark of respect to the Juventus supporters that had perished, and also to those that had died in the Valley Parade fire (see *Grounds For Improvement*). Before kick-off five Englishmen, one of them identified as a member of the National Front, were expelled from the press box. A spokesman for the Mexican football federation said that British journalists pointed them out to Mexican officials. After it was proved that they were not journalists they were escorted to a spectator section in the stadium.

The Newcastle *Sunday Sun* commented on an article by leading sport journalist Bob Harris:

> From Mrs Thatcher downwards so many people have been sharp to condemn Liverpool fans as the lunatics who caused the mayhem in Brussels. But now a different picture is emerging. More and more evidence is being produced to show that there could well be another side to the story and that Liverpool fans are ending up as scapegoats, although not entirely blameless. The Government, the Football Association, the Liverpool FC management have all diverted guilt to supporters who, at the end of the day, could turn out to be a paler shade of grey if not white.

The thrust of Harris's article was that there was a more sinister element to the violence:

> Football supporters, good or bad, tend to wear their colours around their necks and not across their faces like bandits. Were these the people there to watch football? Definitely not. They were to the forefront while they fought the police, but when the successful Juventus team paraded the cup they stood stone-faced, showing no emotion at all.

Harris said that he had seen their ilk at football grounds around the world. He cited many examples and warned that 'the situation has gone far beyond pot-bellied drunks swinging at each other in the name of soccer. They are still there, of course, but now they are unwittingly following a far more sinister element who have seized the opportunity of maximum disruption of civilised society.'

Chapter 20

Grounds for Improvement

> Bolton is a town in mourning today. Flags over the Town Hall and public buildings are flying at half-mast in silent tribute to the Burnden Park football ground tragedy on Saturday.
>
> *Manchester Evening News*

Hillsborough, Heysel, Valley Parade, Ibrox – just some of the stadium names that darken the story of football. Stadiums where fans who had gone to watch a match never returned home. In Ibrox's case, it happened twice, sixty-four years apart. In every case there was a scandal – of football supporters being the victims of inadequate facilities, or of disrepair, or of downright incompetence.

The tragedy that unfolded at Sheffield Wednesday's Hillsborough stadium in April 1989, at the FA Cup semi-final between Liverpool and Nottingham Forest, which ultimately caused the deaths of ninety-seven spectators, was largely attributed to mistakes made by the South Yorkshire police.

The fire at Bradford City's Valley Parade that claimed fifty-six lives on 11 May 1985 came down to a discarded match or cigarette butt setting light to rubbish that had accumulated under the old wooden main stand. One spectator told Mr Justice Popplewell's inquiry into safety at sports grounds that he and a friend had got out of the burning stand through a small store room. Steven Wilkinson said that the stand had been ablaze with people trapped behind the doors. 'People were shouting and screaming for someone to get them out. We pushed against the doors and they came off their hinges and a mass of people came out. The smoke was very thick.'

Just eighteen days after the Bradford fire, thirty-nine fans died at the Heysel Stadium in Brussels (see *The Shame of Heysel*). Those deaths occurred during violent crowd disorder, but even there it was concluded that the fatalities were attributable 'very, very largely due to the appalling state of [the] stadium' that had fallen into a state of disrepair and was long overdue for modernisation.

At Ibrox Park in Glasgow on 5 April 1902, a section of the newly built West Tribune Stand collapsed, leading to the deaths of twenty-five spectators who were among hundreds that fell 12m (40ft) on to a concrete floor below. On 16 September 1961, two people were killed in a crush on a stairway at Ibrox. Although Rangers made improvements, there was more tragedy to follow. On 2 January 1971, sixty-six died in a crush on the same stairway as spectators were leaving the stadium.

And then there was the Burnden Park tragedy of 1946. After six long, war-weary years football was getting back to normal. The Football League would not resume until the 1946–47 season but the FA Cup was under way again, and on 9 March, all roads leading to Burnden Park, home of Bolton Wanderers, were packed. The Trotters were playing host to Stoke City in the second leg of their FA Cup quarter-final tie – for the first and only time in the competition's history, ties up to and including the quarter-finals were played on a two-legged basis with the winners going through on goals aggregate – and the visitors had the great Stanley Matthews in their ranks.

Burnden Park stood on the south side of Bolton, about half a mile from the town centre. Throughout the morning crowds built up in the streets around the ground as supporters arrived early. Home fans queued up, waiting for the turnstiles to open. They were joined by away fans who had arrived on early trains before making the ten-minute walk from the railway station. There was no segregation of rival supporters, no thought of crowd disorder. Everyone had come to see a football match, not to cause trouble.

Bolton held a two-goal advantage from the first leg. Would the home side prevail? Could Matthews, who had spent most of the war guesting for Blackpool where he was stationed in the RAF, turn the tide Stoke's way? Over 85,000 people – some estimates put it as high as 115,000 – wanted to see the outcome at first hand. But the record attendance – and the capacity – for the ground was just under 70,000.

When the gates opened at 1pm, tens of thousands moved forward in orderly fashion to take up their positions on the Burnden Park terraces. However, not everyone was prepared to stand around for hours.

Many could not anyway. First they had factory jobs to do, arriving at Burnden breathless after grabbing a cup of tea and a sandwich before jumping aboard a Bolton Corporation bus to the ground. As kick-off neared, they, too, shuffled their way in. Behind them still more fans flocked towards the stadium that, like almost all football grounds in Britain, had grown from small beginnings in Victorian times and had been extended with no real thought for crowd comfort. Health and safety was not even a work in progress. Thousands more supporters arrived, and the streets became choked as a seething mass of supporters, now growing increasingly anxious about getting in, made their way towards the turnstiles.

By 2.15pm – still forty-five minutes to kick-off – conditions were already becoming uncomfortable both inside and outside the ground. The pressure was now so great around the turnstiles that many would-be spectators were being pushed against the walls of the stadium. On the terraces there was hardly any room to move. Small boys were being passed over adult heads to the front; extricating a bag of sweets or an apple from a jacket pocket became a physical impossibility; keeping one's feet became a priority. Yet still the turnstiles clicked and clattered, feeding more people on to the terraces. Those at the front were being pressed further forward, but it was now impossible to move in any direction.

The streets surrounding the ground were as packed as the terraces inside. There were no police radios; it was impossible for officers in the ground to communicate with those controlling the tens of thousands still hoping to gain admission. A call from a PC Lowe to close the turnstiles reached the head checker too late to make a difference. Discomfort now turned to distress as people began to fall to the ground, and others could not avoid standing on them. With ten minutes to kick-off, the crush outside the turnstiles was relieved almost at a stroke. A spectator, trying to escape the ground with his young son, had managed to open the padlock on a large exit gate designed to spill large numbers back into the streets at the final whistle.

But people were not leaving Burnden Park; thousands more were pouring in. The pressure on the terraces was now unbearable. At five minutes to three, a huge roar signalled the appearance of the teams. On the terraces, tens of thousands of people craned their necks to catch a first glimpse of their favourites. This sea of humanity rolled forward. Most were held in place by a series of strategically placed crush barriers that prevented the swaying masses from pressing down to the front of the terracing.

But there was one area, near the bottom of some steps, where no barriers had been erected. Thousands of people were compressed into this gap, funnelling down uncontrollably. Then barriers elsewhere started to buckle under the strain, and down went the crowd, tumbling forward. Bodies began to pile up, two, three, four deep. Seventy policemen, aided by spectators, and even the linesmen, began the task of pulling people from the heaped pile, and as news spread around the town, doctors were called out and young women from a nearby ATS barracks rushed to the ground.

Twelve minutes into the game, a police sergeant walked on to the pitch and spoke to the referee. George Dutton, of Warwick, stopped play, called the captains, Harry Hubbick of Bolton and Neil Franklin of Stoke, together and then took the teams off the field. The players had to push their way down the tunnel, which was full of spectators seeking refuge, before sitting in their dressing rooms for twenty-five minutes. Word spread that two or three spectators had been killed. Then referee Dutton reappeared, telling the players that, on the advice of the chief constable of Bolton, he was resuming the game. When the teams took the field again, they saw that the pitch had grown smaller. Thousands of spectators were sitting over the original touchline and new markings had been made with sawdust.

At half-time the teams turned straight around with no break. The players were unaware that this was English football's worst tragedy to date: thirty-three people had been killed, over 500 more injured. Best to get the game over with as soon as possible said the officials. It ended goalless, Bolton were through, Stoke were out. That night few people really cared.

One witness, Christopher Stone of Crompton Way in Bolton, said: 'When the crowd began to move forward, I felt as if my ribs were being crushed and I gradually lost consciousness. I found myself being carried over piles of people about four deep.' Another spectator said: 'When the crowd began to surge forward I was lifted off my feet and flung on to the heads of those in front. I saw people on the ground and others sweeping over them.'

The chief constable of Bolton, William Howard, said that about 15,000 people were shut out near the railway embankment entrance, and the police were overwhelmed by thousands rushing to the fence. Sleepers comprising the fence were pulled down, he said, and the great pressure of the massive people surging forward caused two steel crush barriers to collapse.

Howard said that a few days before the match he visited the ground and later two other officers went there to make arrangements for the policing of the match: 'On the day before the match I went over the arrangements with the inspectors and agreed to send 103 men.' He was satisfied that there was a sufficient number that exceeded the number sent to police ordinary matches. Sixty policemen were inside the ground and the rest were outside. Describing his arrival at Burnden Park at 2.25pm, Howard said that conditions in the car park were perfectly orderly. In between the cars were about five orderly queues to the turnstiles. There were the queues in the north-west corner giving admission to the popular embankment enclosure. These were definite queues, he said, and not, as they became later, a solid mass of people.

A Bolton club official said:

> It was a great struggle for the players to have to carry on amid such tragedy, and it was a big decision for the referee to take. But with such a huge crowd unnerved by the awful happenings, it would have been most unwise to abandon the game and might well have led to an even worse disaster. The referee was in a role similar to an orchestra conductor with the theatre on fire – continuing to play in an effort to prevent panic.

A Home Office enquiry chaired by Goronwy 'Ronw' Moelwyn Hughes KC, opened on opened on 28 March 1946. The first witness was Dr G.D. McKenzie, who said that the cause of death in twenty-one cases was asphyxia due to suffocation. 'I don't think any person would have been dead before he had fallen. They were obviously subjected to considerable pressure, so that, once they had fallen, they would probably have succumbed very quickly.'

A father and son, Thomas Robey, aged 55, and Richard Robey, who was 35; two brothers, Fred and James Battersby; and a brother and sister, Frederick Campbell who was 33, and widow Emily Hoskinson who was 40, were among the thirty-three dead. The last to be identified was 56-year-old William Hughes of Wigan, a 6ft-tall man tattooed on both arms. His description had been widely circulated as no inquiry had been made for him.

Dr A.P. Sparks, Stoke City's medical director, was one of the first on the scene. He told a Press Association reporter:

> It was a horrible sight. There was a call for doctors, and I at once went to the St John Ambulance room on the ground. When I reached the immediate point of the tragedy there was just a heaving mass of people, some of whom were already dead. The faces of many who had been thrown to the ground bore the marks of hobnail boots, and socks and stockings of men and women had been torn all to pieces, and they were all covered in dirt.

A Football League spokesman absolved Bolton Wanderers of any blame:

> As it seems that the Bolton club shut the gates I cannot see that any blame attaches to them. They had no control over the people outside the ground, which is entirely a matter for the police. Clubs have no authority over people outside their enclosures. Still, in my experience, no matter how many police you have, when a mob loses its head very little can be done. Only armed and mounted police could stop surges by packed thousands and you would have tragedy anyway. Police anyway are always short-handed nowadays.

The inquiry did indeed find that while the Bolton club and the police had taken proper steps, procedures were inadequate. The real trouble lay in the fact that there had been no scientific assessment of the ground's capacity – this was simply regarded as the greatest number of people to have been safely accommodated there on a previous occasion. There was also no means of knowing when that figure was about to be reached, nor were there facilities for the immediate closing of the turnstiles. An attempt had been made to open exit doors, but the keys could not be found.

The man who had opened the gate to escape with his 12-year-old son, but whose actions had also let in thousands more people, came forward after a police appeal. Norman Chater Crook, a textile engineer from Prestwich, told the inquiry that they had been standing at one end of the embankment enclosure when the crowd began to sway and that it was impossible for his boy, Derek, to see, and so he decided to leave. He couldn't ask to be let out because the turnstile operator was arguing with two men. Mr Crook and his son, 'who was in a pretty bad way', managed to make their way to a gate but found it padlocked. 'I had a bunch of keys in my pocket and unlocked the padlock with one of them, an ordinary screw key.' He went out with his boy and another and mentioned to someone to close the door but did not see it closed. 'There was a sudden rush and when I turned round people were jammed in the door,' he said. He was asked: 'Did you realise when you opened this exit gate that you opened the flood doors that might let in a lot of people?' 'No,' he replied.

Police inspector Herbert Gee said that he saw a soldier being pressed against the railings. He had his arms held helplessly up, so Inspector Gee put the soldier's arms around his neck and heaved him out of the way. People were pulling down the railings to drag people out. Twelve men were working in their spare time as checkers at the turnstiles. One, Jimmy Austin, a railway clerk from Bolton, said: 'I stopped the crowd from outside coming in on my own initiative before I got official orders to close my turnstile.'

Matters had been made worse by the fact that several turnstiles had been rendered unusable, which meant that over 28,000 destined for the Railway Embankment end had to enter from the Manchester Road end. Also, ticket holders for the Burnden Paddock had also been admitted through turnstiles in this area and then escorted around the pitch to their places, adding to the huge build-up in the north-west corner of the ground. In addition to those fans who had poured in when the exit gate was opened by Mr Crook, thousands more had simply climbed over turnstiles and walls. Some had walked along the railway line and down the embankment before breaking into the ground through a fence. One thousand people climbed over the entrance to the boys' enclosure. They had free rein: the police were reluctant to release any officers from the Burnden Stand where they were guarding food stockpiled by the Ministry of Supply.

A relief fund for the injured and their families and those of the dead realised £40,000, and a series of Government recommendations were made so that, in future, football supporters could attend matches in safety. However, many clubs were concerned about the costs of suggestions that Ronw Moelwyn Hughes made to the Home Secretary, James Chuter-Ede, particularly the one that 'mechanical means must be provided to indicate at a central point on football grounds the total of admissions at any moment through all the entrances of enclosures'.

John McMahon, president of the Scottish Football League, and chairman of Clyde FC, said that it would be beyond most football clubs in Scotland to carry out the suggestion if it were decided on. The expense of providing mechanical means to gauge attendances he said would be too great. Bill McCartney, the manager of Hibernian, said that to implement the mechanical-means suggested would be 'utterly impossible'.

Will Cearns, a member of the Football League management committee and the managing director of Wimbledon greyhound racing stadium, raised the subject of all-ticket football matches: 'Admission only by a ticket obtained beforehand, as in the big matches at Wembley and Hampden Park, and the division of standing terraces into pens, seems the surest way of preventing a repetition.' But then he added: 'All-ticket matches act as a big deterrent to people who hoped to get in on the off-chance of there being room. But even then you could never be certain that ticketless enthusiasts would not try to break into the ground.'

Despite the huge amount of money pouring into the game through the turnstiles in the post-war years, when players were still on a maximum wage, little was spent on ground improvements. It was indeed a scandal that would continue to cost lives on British football grounds and elsewhere.

Twenty-four hours after the Burnden Park tragedy, several people were injured, four of them seriously with spinal injuries and fractures, at another cup-tie when pressure from the crowd pushed over a concrete boundary wall. During the FAI Cup quarter-final second-leg match between Shamrock Rovers and Dundalk at Milltown in Dublin on 10 March 1946, about 90ft of the wall separating the pitch from the general enclosure gave way. It was the second time in less than six weeks that the wall had given way. The match was delayed while loudspeakers called for people with cars to take the injured to hospital. Meanwhile Shamrock Rovers went through to the semi-finals. Again, the question was asked: was it right to continue? Some people thought that a scandal.

Bibliography

Books

Ford, Trevor, *I Lead The Attack!,* Stanley Paul, 1957
Hapgood, Eddie, *Football Ambassador*, Sporting Handbooks, 1945
Hewitt, Ian, *Sporting Justice*, Sports Books, 2008
Inglis, Simon, *Soccer In The Dock*, Willow Books, 1985
Lawton, Tommy, *Football Is My Business*, Sporting Handbooks, 1946
Lennox, Bobby (with Gerry McNee), *A Million Miles For Celtic*, Stanley Paul, 1982
Matthews, Stanley, *The Stanley Matthews Story*, Oldbourne Book Co Ltd, 1960
Morrison, Ian, *The World Cup: A Complete Record*, Breedon Books, 1990
Rippon, Anton, *Gas Masks For Goalposts*, Sutton Publishing, 2005
Schumacher, Toni, *Blowing The Whistle*, W.H. Allen, 1987
Ward, Andrew, *Soccer's Strangest Matches*, Robson Books, 1989

Newspapers and magazines

Aberdeen Press and Journal
Athletic News
Belfast Telegraph
Birmingham Post
Clarín
Daily Express
Daily Herald
Daily Mail
(Sheffield) *Daily Independent*
Diario
Diario 16

Dublin Evening Herald
East Anglian Daily Times
El Comercio
El Dia
El Mercurio
El Pais
El Popular
La Gazetta Dello Sport
Hertford Mercury and Reformer
Irish Independent
La Derniere Heure
La Mañana
La Provence
La Tercera
Le Nouvel Observateur
L'Equipe
L'Éxpress
Lincolnshire Echo
Liverpool Echo
Manchester Courier
Manchester Evening News
Marca
New Civil Engineer
News Chronicle
Nottingham Evening Post
Oxford Chronicle and Reading Gazette Sporting Chronicle
Sporting Chronicle
Sunday Mirror
(Newcastle) *Sunday Sun*
(Dublin) *Sunday Tribune*
The Economist
The Observer
The People
The Sun
Veja
Walsall Observer
Western Daily Press
Zeit Magazine

Index